Swashbuckling Faith

TIM WESEMANN

D0062926

Multnomah ® Publishers *Sisters, Oregon*

SWASHBUCKLING FAITH

published by Multnomah Publishers, Inc.

© 2006 by Tim Wesemann

International Standard Book Number: 1-59052-704-6

Cover image by Erich Lessing/Art Resource, NY

Unless otherwise indicated, Scripture quotations are from:

The Holy Bible, New International Version © 1973, 1984 by International Bible Society, used by permission of Zondervan Publishing House

Other Scripture quotations are from:

The Message by Eugene H. Peterson, Copyright © 1993, 1994, 1995, 1996, 2000. Used by permission of NavPress Publishing Group. All rights reserved.

The Holy Bible, King James Version (KJV)

Multnomah is a trademark of Multnomah Publishers, Inc., and is registered in the U.S. Patent and Trademark Office. The colophon is a trademark of Multnomah Publishers, Inc.

Printed in the United States of America

For information:

MULTNOMAH PUBLISHERS, INC.
601 N. LARCH STREET
SISTERS, OREGON 97759

LIBRARY OF CONGRESS CATALOGING-IN-PUBLICATION DATA

Wesemann, Tim, 1960-

Swashbuckling faith / Tim Wesemann.

    p. cm.

ISBN 1-59052-704-6

1. Christian life. 2. Pirates of the Caribbean, the curse of the black pearl (Motion picture)—Miscellanea. I. Title.

BV4501.3.W425 2006

248.4—dc22

2006008130

06 07 08 09 10—10 9 8 7 6 5 4 3 2 1 0

For
Benjamin, Sarah, and Christopher—
I'd walk the plank for you any day, mates.
I love you!
DAD

MIKE
In the words of Commodore Norrington:
"I believe thanks are in order."

Contents

Acknowledgments

My Captain, setting sail on this writing adventure with You has been pure joy. You set the course, assembled the crew, and gladly revealed heaven's treasures. It's always an honor to serve You, my Captain. Your grace shivers me faith timbers.

O ye splendid and gifted editor, Steffany Woolsey: What a pleasure to sail with you on this treasure hunt. I appreciate your Christ-centered heart of joy and encouragement. Now get back to swabbing the decks of those manuscripts!

Major league kudos to the entire Multnomah team—what a fun and amazing group, including Tim, Jodi, Mandy, Kimberly, that guy over there, and that young lady in the cubby. I'm so impressed with everyone, I should even thank the janitorial team! (By the way, editorial staff, I'm still waiting for my cut of the winning treasure from the costume party!)

My most excellent and influential agent, Steve Laube: It's always good to have you in the crow's nest, pointing out the smooth waters ahead.

Benjamin, Sarah, Christopher, and Chiara: What a crew! Thank you for putting up with me while I sat at the computer wearing my official Jack Sparrow costume. I'm so glad we're traveling together because we can't accomplish much all by our onesies! Always remember that not all treasure is silver and gold, mates.

Judy Rehmer: I hope you believe in (Holy) Ghost stories, because you're in one! Thank you for allowing God's Spirit to guide your edits, input, and encouragement.

Cathy and Dave, Ted and Jane, Don and Diane: Ahoy, family! I told you I'd find a way to include your names in this book!

Mom and Dad: Our Captain will pass on my love and thanks as you feast together at His heavenly table.

My friends, prayer partners, and encouragers: Your friendship filled the sails with a heavenly breeze, keeping this ship moving forward. Special thanks to the crew of friends on the *Servants of the Caribbean* Trinidad Mission Team.

Introduction

Surrounded by redcoats, Commodore James Norrington addresses the pirate with open contempt: "Well, well. Jack Sparrow, isn't it?"

"Captain Jack Sparrow, if you please, sir."

Norrington examines Jack's one-bullet pistol, his compass that doesn't point to magnetic north, and his pirate's sword. Then he looks into Jack's eyes and says, "You are without a doubt the worst pirate I've ever heard of."

Jack fires back: "But you have heard of me."

Now, you should know that I'm not a pirate, nor do I play one on TV. I am a Christian who loves to find biblical truths in daily life—including movies with pirates who pillage, plunder, and pilfer.

Millions of people know of Jack Sparrow (pardon me, make that *Captain* Jack Sparrow), who confessed his intention to commandeer a British ship, pick up a crew in Tortuga, and commence with some raiding, pillaging, and plundering.

Ah, yes…it's a pirate's life for Captain Jack Sparrow. And with the popularity of the *Pirates of the Caribbean* movies, it's safe to say that a *lot* of people are familiar with this pirate named Jack.

You might be surprised to hear that the charcoal-eyed, straggly haired pirate also taught me quite a bit about Christian living. Yep, mate, thar's a treasure trove of faith-growing gems waiting to be discovered within the movie, sparkling vibrantly as the Light reflects from each facet. *Swashbuckling Faith* uses the treasure map of God's Word to explore these life-changing gems.

With the help of the Holy Spirit, we'll become swashbucklers ourselves—explorers who will fight for the treasure, cross blades for truth, and duel for the One who gives us life. That's swashbuckling faith.

Before we raise the anchor and head out to sea in anticipation of adventure, let's climb to the crow's nest. From there we can see what lies ahead as we sail toward the heavenly horizon.

While I am a fan of the *Pirates of the Caribbean* movies, let me state the obvious: They're not Christian flicks. This book is not an endorsement of the movie, nor am I affiliated with it in any way.

As a former parish pastor, and now a full-time Christian author and speaker, I love how God leads us through the treasure map of His Word to discover faith riches. I'm so glad the divine Captain invited you to join me on this adventure in search of life treasure.

Jesus often used the same approach in growing faith in His followers as He walked the earth (and sea). He understood the culture and wanted to meet people where they were, so He used stories and familiar objects to inform them about the kingdom.

In much the same way, Paul—make that the *apostle* Paul—when visiting Athens (Acts 17) used its idol-junkie culture and worship, including an altar with the inscription "To an Unknown God," to present the gospel in a creative way.

The same cultural treasure chest is available to us today. Unexpected faith treasures are at our fingertips. The treasures aren't even hidden. The Holy Spirit wants us to see and seize the treasures. The rough seas come when pirate ships waving their flags of temptation attack our belief in the riches of God's grace. Thankfully, our Captain leads us safely through the storms.

So climb aboard! The wind's at our back, and treasure awaits. As Jack Sparrow once said, "Now, bring me that horizon."

Take Yer Hat Off to Those Gone Before Ye

PIRATES HOOK

The pirate's long, unkempt black hair blows loosely beneath his worn tricorn hat. One hand rests on his hip; the other grasps the crow's nest of his craft.

Captain Jack Sparrow, carefree pirate.

The pirate has a sinking feeling that something has run amok. He glances down. His confidence turns to panic—understandably so, since the hull of his vessel is taking in more than a little water.

Grabbing loose rigging, Jack bounds down from his perch, splashing into the flooded hull. He seizes a wooden bucket and begins bailing.

Captain Jack Sparrow, self-sufficient pirate.

Jack suddenly spots a gibbet stretched between two trees on the shoreline. Three hanged pirates sway gently from their nooses. A crude wooden sign reads, "Pirates— Ye Been Warned!"

Jack tosses aside the bucket, places his hat over his heart, and offers the departed pirates a moment of reverent silence.

Captain Jack Sparrow, respectful pirate (if not always respected).

DISCOVERING THE TREASURE

I love that part of *Pirates of the Caribbean* when Jack Sparrow ceases bailing water to stand at attention for those lifeless pirates hanging from the gallows. That move is classic Captain Jack: stopping to honor those who sailed before him, even in the midst of a crisis.

I should do that more often.

I'm thankful for a variety of heroes God placed in my life. Jack Buck, for instance—one of my baseball heroes. Although he wasn't a player, he brought the game to life for me through the radio. During his career, Jack Buck memorialized hundreds of calls for fans in St. Louis and across America. My favorite line is something he once said after a record-breaking home run: "Pardon me while I stand up and applaud!"

I thought about that line when Captain Jack Sparrow stood in his sinking ship and, in his own way, applauded his fellow departed pirates by removing his hat and placing it over his heart.

I too have many spiritual heroes that helped pave my way to the cross—people God used to shape me into the person I am today. My grandfather Conrad is one of those heroes. I wasn't born until three months after he died, so I never met Conrad— yet his life deeply impacted mine.

Like Jack Sparrow, Conrad spent a great deal of time on the water—but his adventures took him farther south than the Caribbean.

In 1913 Conrad and his wife, Magdalena, boarded a ship headed for southern Brazil. They were taking the gospel to the people of that area. (Just in case you're wondering, they did *not* encounter pirate ships when they passed through Caribbean waters.)

In the years following, Conrad held at least fourteen mission posts. He made his rounds on horseback, by canoe, and sometimes afoot, often separated from his family for months at a time. In the seventeen years he spent in Brazil, the Bible served as Conrad's treasure map.

Conrad and Magdalena, when I consider the story of your lives and ministries, these words come to mind: *Pardon me while I stand up and applaud!*

Then there are my great-grandparents, who raised their children in the Christian faith and instilled within them a passion to spread the treasure around the world. Johann and Katharina, *pardon me while I stand up and applaud!*

So many heroes hang around the cross that bears a rickety, hand-lettered sign telling all who pass by that the one on that cross is Jesus. The sign doesn't say "Beware!" like the one Jack Sparrow saw; rather, "Be Aware!" To the millions who have arrived in heaven before me, leaving behind a part of the treasure…

Pardon me while I stand up and applaud!

The interesting thing is that those same people, as well as unnamed millions more—all veterans of the cross—are on your list too. Check out these verses:

Do you see what this means—all these pioneers who blazed the way, all these veterans cheering us on?

It means we'd better get on with it. Strip down, start running—and never quit! No extra spiritual fat, no parasitic sins. Keep your eyes on Jesus, who both began and finished this race we're in. Study how he did it. Because he never lost sight of where he was headed—that exhilarating finish in and with God— he could put up with anything along the way: cross, shame, whatever. And now he's there, in the place of honor, right alongside God. When you find yourselves flagging in your faith, go over that story again, item by item, that long litany of hostility he plowed through. That will shoot adrenaline into your souls! (Hebrews 12:1–3, *The Message*)

Glowing superlatives can't do justice to the gift of Jesus, the gift of life, the gift of empowerment, the gift of heaven, the gift of God working through the cloud of witnesses that surrounds us.

Pardon me while I stand up and applaud!

Close your eyes for a moment.

Listen. Just listen.

(Silence)

Do you hear them?

They're right there. Around you. The great cloud of witnesses, the faithful pioneers God used to blaze the way, the veterans of the faith—they're cheering you on.

But we're not done applauding. We must consider something—and Someone—else.

Consider him who endured such opposition from sinful men, so that you will not grow weary and lose heart. (Hebrews 12:3)

Looking from the outside in, one can assume that Jesus knew what it was like to helm a sinking ship. Think about it: Crises popped up almost everywhere He went. People begged Him for healing. Satan tempted Him. Family members rejected Him. Friends died. Hungry people needed His attention. Enemies ambushed Him. His friends couldn't get along. Demons cried out to Him. A close friend betrayed Him. He received a death sentence.

Then consider this encouragement from Hebrews 12:3. If you're using the JSV translation of the Bible (that's the Jack Sparrow Version), you might find it written this way:

Consider Jesus when yer faith be sinkin'. Quit tryin' t' bail yerself ou' o' th' mess. He's th' one who will bail ye ou'. In th' middle o' yer crisis, consider what He sailed through fer ye. Look around ye. Be seein' an' hearin' th' faithful crew members who be havin' gone before ye. Get t' yer feet. Remember. Give thanks. Receive th' glory strength yer Savior has fer ye. Be encouraged by th' cheerin' faithful. That'll put wind in yer sails.

The JSV ain't so bad, aye?

When we consider Jesus and all He sailed through for us, we confirm that the Holy Spirit uses our Savior's faithfulness, example, and love to put wind in our sails.

The blind begged for healing, which sent pious
    ones reeling.
Crowds closed Him in, needing forgiveness for sin.
His kin withheld honor, yet them He still honored.
Many mocked His claims—for those He came.
He dined with the outcasts whom the chief priests had
    cast out.
The sick needed attention; His own needed direction.
Peter lied, then denied.
A disciple betrayed; the Pharisees preyed.

People despised Him; Pilate tried Him.
Some abused Him; many used Him.
He was beaten to death, so death wouldn't beat us.
He gave Satan hell, and to us He gave heaven.
Sinless, He received a death sentence;
Sinful, we receive a life sentence.

Pardon me while I stand up and applaud!

I Believe Thanks Are in Order

PIRATES HOOK

Coughing up seawater, Elizabeth catches her breath and steadies herself near her rescuer, Jack Sparrow. Instantly, redcoats swarm the rescue dock along with Elizabeth's governor father and the pursuer of her heart, Commodore Norrington.

Without waiting for discussion, the Commodore calls for Jack's head.

But Elizabeth, capable of turning a head or two of her own, rushes to her rescuer's defense—a strategy that temporarily softens Norrington's heart.

Extending his hand to Jack, he speaks with some disdain: "I believe thanks are in order."

A heart of thanks portrayed by a friendly gesture? Hardly. Norrington wanted proof Jack was a pirate. The tattoo on Jack's extended forearm provided it.

DISCOVERING THE TREASURE

I consider myself a generally thankful person. When thanks are in order, I usually share them. In fact, just today I thanked the restaurant hostess who showed me to a table, as well as the server who let me substitute mashed potatoes for the vegetable medley. When I merged into the left lane, I thanked drivers who let me in with a friendly wave. I even thanked the grand-mother on crutches with four packages and three grandbabies hanging on her as she held the door open for me at the mall. (Relax, I'm joking. She had only two grandbabies, not three.) My point is, I truly do enjoy thanking others.

By the way, have I thanked you for buying this book, along with five additional copies to give your family and friends? If I failed to do so, please know I'm extremely grateful.

Are you thinking I had an ulterior motive in thanking you just now?

Thanks can be insincere or contain a hidden motivation. That's what happened in the opening scene to our friendly Jack Sparrow. When Jack rescued Elizabeth from drowning, Norrington offered Jack his hand in gratitude—but as you saw, Norrington's motives were ill-conceived.

It's easy to thank someone who compliments us on wearing the latest in pirate formal wear, or a coworker who helps us swab the deck, or even a stranger who offers directions to Tortuga.

Unfortunately, we often forget to let significant people in our lives know how grateful we are for how they've impacted us. These include:

- parents who make sacrifices
- kids that bring out the kid in us

- family members who love us unconditionally
- friends who encourage us
- pastors who hold true to God's Word when teaching us
- teachers who fill our minds with knowledge and hearts with compassion
- caregivers who serve our needs
- siblings who put up with us

Did I miss anyone?

Ah, yes. The One who is all that and much more. The One who became the perfect sacrifice to save us, who brings out childlike faith in His children. The One who encourages and teaches us.

His name is Jesus.

Consider just a few example of Jesus taking time to thank His Father: prior to the feeding of the thousands (Matthew 15:36); in the Upper Room, when He instituted what we know as the Lord's Supper (Matthew 26:26); and when He raised Lazarus from the dead (John 11:41).

But how many situations can you think of where someone specifically thanked Jesus? The tenth leper comes to mind (Luke 17:11–19), when Jesus healed ten but only one returned to thank him.

Got any more? I searched the Scriptures but didn't find other examples.

That's sad, don't you think?

Obviously, just because it isn't recorded in Scripture doesn't mean people didn't thank Jesus. Besides, there are numerous scriptural references to a person or group praising God for what Jesus did in their midst, and praise and thankfulness do go hand in hand. Still, I find the lack of purposeful thanks interesting, even disturbing, since Jesus spent His life serving others. You would think the Gospel accounts of Jesus' life would overflow with words of thanks in response to His goodness, wouldn't you?

Now, before I go pointing my hook at others, I have to stop and recognize that it's curled up and pointing right back at me. My lack of thankfulness sends me running to the cross-beam—not the one on the mast; the one on which our Master hangs while winning the duel with the devil. It's there that we receive the gift of forgiveness.

Consider this: Jesus walked the plank in our place. Well, shiver me timbers! If that doesn't cause you to give thanks, what will?

Let's set sail on a course of thanksgiving! The barnacles of sin slowing us down have been scraped away.

What's that? You say it would take an eternity to thank God for all His blessings? Ah, good idea—very good idea! No doubt an eternity of thanks is in order.

Look around you and just try to keep from feeling thankful! Then let that thanks sail upward and outward freely. I'll give you a push off the dock if you need one...

Lord Jesus, Your heart overflows blessings into my life, causing my thanks to spill over. Nothing You do is insignificant. Nothing should go unnoticed. My Savior, thanks are more than in order.

Thank You, gracious Lord, for...

✠ *alarm clocks with snooze buttons and snoozers that don't snore.*

✠ *warm, fluffy slippers and opportunities to slip into old, worn-out jeans.*

✠ pants with elastic waists and days off full of time to waste.

✠ indoor plumbing and people plum full of ideas.

✠ hearts that beat and deals that can't be beat.

✠ big bear hugs and little tugs on your sleeve you can't bear to ignore.

✠ regular trash pickup and spiritual pick-me-ups.

✠ baby coos and honey-dos.

✠ catnaps and fat cats.

✠ belly laughs and the jokes that produce them.

✠ chocolate and…well, chocolate should stand alone.

✠ paychecks and paid-off loans.

✠ microwaves and ocean waves.

✠ invocations and benedictions (and everything in between).

✠ things you sink your teeth into and Grandpa's teeth sitting next to the sink.

✠ angel protection and angelic relationships worth protecting.

✠ eyes for seeing, ears for hearing, and appendixes for doing whatever they do.

✠ family united by blood and family bonded by the blood of Jesus.

✠ grace du jour and a Savior who takes that grace and feeds the multitudes.

In the words of Commodore Norrington, I believe thanks are in order.

Thank You, Jesus.

*Captain,
if You Please*

PIRATES HOOK

Like a vice-squad detective searching for needle marks on a junkie, Commodore Norrington shoves Jack's sleeve up his forearm. He finds needle marks, all right—the ones used to make the tattoo that labels Jack a pirate.

Norrington slides Jack's sleeve up even farther, revealing a second tattoo. This one, of a bird flying over the ocean, exposes the pirate's identity.

"Well, well. Jack Sparrow, isn't it?" the Commodore sneers.

Polite but defiant, Jack responds, "Captain Jack Sparrow, if you please."

DISCOVERING THE TREASURE

What title do people use to address you? Mister, missus, miss, Doctor, Nurse, Teacher, Reverend, Pastor, sir, ma'am, Mom,

Dad, Punkin Doodle, Your Honor, Your Holiness, or even King? (Hey, you never know who might be reading.) Some of us have worked hard to achieve titles that we value highly, while others prefer to go by their names or even nicknames.

Personally, I'm not hung up on titles. I remember the first time some young scalawag called me *Mister*. I was working at a gardening shop at the time. Come to find out, he wanted me to hand him the mister.... Okay, I just made that up. But you get my point.

Don't get me wrong, I believe it's good and godly to respect others, and if that includes addressing them with a title, great. But all I really care about is that when the roll is called up yonder, I hear my name—no titles attached!

Captain Jack Sparrow obviously relishes the title *Captain*. It was bestowed upon him when he captained the *Black Pearl*, back before the mutiny (but that's another story). The point is, the title *Captain* gives Jack an identity and commands others' respect (well, sometimes).

Even now, without a ship, Jack will not be stripped of his title. It connects him to his past and provides hope for his future.

Jack certainly isn't the first person with a title that connects to the past while providing hope for the future. Take the name of the Lord, for example. Have you ever noticed how the word Lord is set in small caps throughout most of the Old Testament? That stylistic touch is easy to overlook, but Lord is a title—a name—we can't ignore. It adds much to the history of His story and the relationship we enjoy with Him. Let's consider how.

If you could buy a special Captain Jack Sparrow spyglass powerful enough to see through words on a page, you would discover treasure within the word Lord. Behind those four capitalized letters are four Hebrew letters: YHWH. Still don't see the treasure? YHWH, in English, is Yahweh.

Sit tight, there's more! In Exodus 3:15, God tells Moses and the Israelites to call Him by His *personal* name, YHWH or Yahweh.

In other words, God wants to get up close and personal. Savvy?

Come aboard with me for a short side trip to Hebrewland. We'll sail slowly from port to port, collecting treasures as we go. If we remain on course, I believe a great treasure awaits our growing faith.

Port #1

The Hebrew name *Elohim* is a somewhat general name for God (by general, I certainly don't mean it commands less respect).

Port #2

The Hebrew word *Adonai* serves as another name for *Lord* (as in *My Lord and Master*).

Port #3

Yahweh, noted in the Bible as *LORD*, is the personal covenant name for God.

To me, the fact that God tells His people to call Him by His personal name is like a port in the storm.

The Israelites must have been floored when Moses shared this message from God:

"Say to the Israelites, 'The LORD, the God of your fathers—the God of Abraham, the God of Isaac and the God of Jacob—has sent me to you.' This is my name forever, the name by which I am to be remembered from generation to generation." (Exodus 3:15)

How did they rate permission to call the God of the universe by His personal name? And who are we to do the same?

Great questions. The name *Yahweh* gives us the answer. By inviting us to use that name, God lets us know that our relationship with Him is so valuable that He wants us to call Him by His personal name.

Think about it. A child doesn't call his parents Mr. Dad and Mrs. Mom. A doctor's wife doesn't call her husband Dr. So-and-So.

On the other hand, if you don't have a close relationship with someone, you likely use the appropriate title...*until you are invited to use a personal name.*

Back to the question of how we rate permission to call the God of the universe by His personal name. It's a gift—a confirmation of the intimate relationship He wants us to enjoy with Him. If you think about that, it truly is astonishing.

God made a covenant with His people to love and save them. As they called Him Yahweh, they were reminded of and encouraged by His unfailing love and covenant promise. And this same personal relationship is God's enduring gift to His people through the ages. We're in the same boat as the rest of God's people, both past and present.

Reading the word LORD in Scripture lends a new dimension to God's actions described there. Go ahead, flip to almost any page of the Old Testament and find the name LORD (in small caps).

For example, check out the first three verses of Psalm 18:

I love you, O LORD, my strength.
The LORD is my rock, my fortress and my deliverer;

my God is my rock, in whom I take refuge.
He is my shield and the horn of my salvation,
my stronghold.
I call to the LORD, who is worthy of praise, and I
am saved from my enemies.

Now read them again. But this time, when you read *LORD*, consider the intimacy behind the name. This is the Lord with whom both you and the psalmist David have a personal relationship. This is the King of all creation, the almighty, everlasting God who not only knows you but is crazy in love with you. He invites you to come into His presence and call Him by His personal name, His covenant name.

He reminds you of His faithfulness in your past, His unfathomable grace in the present, and His unwavering promises for your future.

Yahweh, your God.

Stand in wonder at the name.

Yahweh, your personal Savior.

Celebrate the relationship.

Yahweh, your LORD.

Take it personally. Take it *very* personally.

One Good Deed Deserves...

PIRATES HOOK

One good deed is not enough to redeem a man of a lifetime of wickedness.

Come on, Commodore. Jack saved her life!

One good deed is not enough to redeem a man of a lifetime of wickedness.

Listen to the sweet pleas of the one you want as your sweet-pea bride...please?

One good deed is not enough to redeem a man of a lifetime of wickedness.

Commodore, is your wig cutting off blood flow to your brain? Captain Jack Sparrow is a simple man who travels with a compass that doesn't point north and a gun with only one bullet. He's the Barney Fife of piratedom, and you're the big bad bully. What harm can he do?

One good deed is not enough to redeem a man of a lifetime of wickedness...though it seems enough to condemn Jack.

Indeed.

DISCOVERING THE TREASURE

Norrington isn't about to let Jack Sparrow sail off into the sunset when he has the swashbuckler in his grasp.

He doesn't care that Jack donned the hero's hat and saved Elizabeth, nor that the lass herself is begging that Jack's life be saved in return. The newly promoted Commodore can't get past the thought that the man before him spent his life pillaging and plundering. Besides, ridding his townspeople of a despicable character would be a feather in his commodorian hat, so to speak. That's why he turns down Elizabeth's request to pardon the man who saved her life.

Why should one good act redeem Jack from a lifetime of iniquities?

Maybe a better question is whether one good act should redeem *us* from a lifetime of iniquity. The answer to that question lies in another story…a true story about a Savior named Jesus. Let's explore for that treasure by looking at the end of Jesus' life on earth.

The Pharisees and Sadducees weren't about to let thousands of people follow Jesus into the Galilean sunset when they had Him within their grasp. They didn't care that the people put a hero's hat on Jesus because of His miraculous and authoritative ways; those legalistic and pious religious leaders couldn't get past the thought that the man before them had spent His life acting like God's gift to mankind. Besides, ridding the country of this heretical yet popular newcomer would be a feather in their self-righteous hats, so to speak. That's why they turned down requests to pardon the One who, unbeknownst to them, came to save their lives.

Why should a few miraculous acts redeem Jesus from a lifetime of drawing people to Himself?

The death-to-the-prophet mantra of the Pharisees reached its peak when Jesus raised Lazarus from the dead. Many of the Jews who witnessed that miracle put their faith in Jesus. Realizing things were getting out of their control, the chief priests and Pharisees called an emergency closed-door meeting. They didn't want subcommittees, task forces, or focus groups formed (in stark contrast to today's congregational meetings!). There was no time to waste. Desperate times called for desperate measures. Besides, they were shaking in their sandals.

Eliminating Jesus was the only item on the agenda. The discussion went like this: "If we let him go on like this, everyone will believe in him, and then the Romans will come and take away both our place and our nation" (John 11:48).

Then Caiaphas, the chief priest, took charge of the situation. "Can't you see that it's to our advantage that one man dies for the people rather than the whole nation be destroyed?" (John 11:50, *The Message*).

The room buzzed. We already know from Scripture that one good, sinless man would soon die in the place of an entire world. But that knowledge was still unbeknownst to Caiaphas, whose words foretold Jesus' death. Caiaphas essentially said, "One good man deserves to die instead of an entire nation."

Don't you love the way God works? Caiaphas had no idea that what he said would come true—and in a way he couldn't even imagine.

Scripture tells us that from that time on the religious leaders plotted to kill Jesus (John 11:53). Little did they know that God's plan was already in motion! Jesus would die for the salvation of the world—one perfect deed.

An old adage says, *One good turn deserves another.*

Jesus' enthusiastic response? *One good turn gives praise to My Father in heaven.*

Caiaphas says, *One good man deserves to die instead of an entire nation.*

Jesus' prophecy fulfilled: *One good, sinless man* did *die in the place of an entire world.*

Commodore Norrington says, *One good deed is not enough to redeem a man of a lifetime of wickedness.*

Jesus' grace-filled response: *One good deed is enough to redeem the world of a lifetime of wickedness.*

Amazingly, Jesus paid the price with His own life, His own bloody sacrifice. He made the purchase, and we're the ones who receive His gift of grace.

God's gifts are all around. There's forgiveness over there…and look at that one—heaven! He took lots of time on the gift of hope. Peace comes wrapped in contentment. That Caiaphas-colored present contains the truth that God often works through people who don't have our best in mind. The keepsake in that gift bag reminds us to let our all-knowing Lord guide our plans. And there's a miraculous present that Lazarus could have helped Jesus wrap—resurrection.

And check out the size of that last one. What beautiful wrapping paper. Let's tear into it. Yes! Just what we wanted, just what we need—life. Abundant life overflowing with more hand-me-downs. There must be a million gifts here. All handmade, all wrapped in compassion. All handed down from heaven by a Savior who reached out in love, allowing Roman nails to pierce them.

Gifts as far as the eye can see. They're all under the tree… the tree in the shape of a cross.

One cross.

One good deed.

One perfect sacrifice.
One flawless redemption.
One overwhelming gift.
One sinless life.
One death.
One man.
One certain hope.
One living Savior.
One good deed of grace.
One life-changing, life-giving deed.
One good deed that deserves a lifetime of gratitude.
One gift that keeps on giving.

Remember the Day

PIRATES HOOK

An angry Commodore Norrington, an anxious Governor, and an apprehensive Elizabeth stand before a faction of redcoats who are armed and ready to do away with Captain Jack Sparrow.

First, though, Norrington and the redcoats must deal with a minor problem.

Jack is positioned behind Elizabeth and is using her as a shield. One can almost see the cogs of Jack's mind turning as he plots his escape. To be sure, he's escaped far worse situations. This should be a piece of cake.

And so, before putting his plan into action, he boasts, "Gentlemen, m'lady, you will always remember this as the day you almost caught Captain Jack Sparrow."

With that, he shoves Elizabeth toward the crowd and uses the ship's rigging to flee the scene.

After running through town, hiding wherever possible, and even engaging in a brief swordfight, Jack realizes that his grand escape will be short-lived.

He soon finds himself recaptured by Norrington and his redcoat shadows, who are anxious to throw him into a jail cell where he can await a break-of-dawn meeting with the gallows.

Norrington mocks the pirate: "I trust you will remember this as the day Captain Jack Sparrow almost escaped."

DISCOVERING THE TREASURE

Perhaps you remember certain days like…

- the first day of school
- Christmas Days gone by
- the day the Holy Spirit created faith in you
- your first date
- the day(s) you got in trouble at school
- graduation day
- the day a family member or friend died
- the day you purchased your first car
- the first day of college
- your first day on the job
- your wedding day
- the birthday of a child
- yesterday

Memories of both good and bad days fill our heads and hearts. They're really all we know, aren't they? The present we live in lasts for only a millisecond before it becomes a memory.

Think how short that millisecond is to God, who thinks in terms of eternity. Maybe that's why God is big on remembering.

In fact, remembering is a common theme throughout the Bible. The word *remember* appears 162 times in the NIV translation of the Bible. Many of those passages tell us that God remembers forever.

> [The Lord said,] I will remember my covenant between me and you and all living creatures of every kind. Never again will the waters become a flood to destroy all life. (Genesis 9:15)

In other instances, people plead with God to remember His faithful promises.

> Remember, O LORD, your great mercy and love, for they are from of old. (Psalm 25:6)
> Then he said, "Jesus, remember me when you come into your kingdom." (Luke 23:42)

Sometimes, but not nearly often enough, God's people remember Him.

> They remembered that God was their Rock, that God Most High was their Redeemer. (Psalm 78:35)

On other occasions, God asks His people to remember His promises as they come together in faith.

> The Lord Jesus, on the night he was betrayed, took bread, and when he had given thanks, he broke it and said, "This is my body, which is for you; do this in remembrance of me."

In the same way, after supper he took the cup, saying, "This cup is the new covenant in my blood; do this, whenever you drink it, in remembrance of me." (1 Corinthians 11:23–25)

I believe that God intends for us to look at His past faithfulness for our future hope. We thank Him for helping us get beyond past sins through His forgiveness. We celebrate how He has brought us through difficulties and hurts. Do you remember those days of hurt? Do you remember how you found peace during them? Do you think God showed you the way?

Do you also remember past situations that propel you toward the future? Remember when...

- you were freed from the shackles of guilt through His forgiveness?
- you realized that He will never leave you or forsake you?
- you began to long for heaven instead of fearing it?
- you heard Jesus whisper *Do not fear*—and trusted Him?
- you took hold of God's promise to you in Romans 8:28 to take whatever life hands you and shape something good from it?
- you felt peace that truly surpasses all understanding?
- you first felt yourself lifted up by Christ through your Spirit-given faith?
- you grasped the reality that you cannot earn your way into heaven—that you are saved by grace through faith in Jesus Christ?

- you understood what it means to be a part of the body of Christ, His church?
- you realized Jesus will not go back on any of His promises?
- you fully trusted that when Jesus forgives your sins, He also promises to forget them completely?
- you found rest in the arms of Jesus?
- you really started living—Christ's way?

Does remembering give you strength to face what is to come?

Remember, this is the day the Lord has made—a day He isn't about to let you escape from His promises or from true life in Him. Jesus said, "I have come that they may have life, and have it to the full" (John 10:10).

I trust you'll be content to let Jesus (not Commodore Norrington) take you away with Him into the future, where He'll continue to remain faithful to *all* His promises.

Are you ready to move into the future, second by second, hour by hour, day by day?

Take me away, Savior.
Take me forward in faith.
Take me forward, trusting.
I am ready.
Lead the way.
May past faithfulness carry me into a bright tomorrow filled with Your amazing, freeing grace.
Create in me Christ-filled memories to last a lifetime…and beyond.
Take me away, Jesus.

Fancy the Footwork

PIRATES HOOK

Dodging the enemy stealthily, Jack makes his way through the streets of Port Royal, eventually ducking into the blacksmith shop. He thinks he's stumbled upon a temporary haven, but quickly finds out differently when through the door walks Will Turner, accomplished swordmaker and master swordfighter.

Jack is not intimidated… but then, neither does he realize just whom he's up against.

And of course it doesn't cross Will's mind to yield to the pirate.

Eyes lock. Blades cross. Steel meets steel. Bodies align. Sword arms flex, strong and prepared.

You think this wise, boy—crossing blades with a pirate?

Will extends his sword. Jack recovers and evades. A parry is followed swiftly by a sidestep. The duo's swordsmanship skills are flawless. Jack acknowledges this by saying, "You know what you're doing, I'll give you that. Excellent form. But how's your footwork?"

Jack, left foot over right, glides easily to his right. Will follows with a sidestep in synchronized fashion, the steel in his hand continuing to cross Jack's. Step by step, the men move uniformly. Each blade blocks the swash of the other until finally Jack lunges forward, causing Will's sword arm to fall by his side.

With that, Jack bids his opponent a glib good-bye—"Ta!"—and bounds for the door.

DISCOVERING THE TREASURE

According to several reports, Michael Flatley of Riverdance fame set a world record several years ago for his fast footwork—an amazing 35 taps per second.

That's some fancy footwork!

I found myself wondering how close I could come to his record, so I gave it a shot. I averaged 3.5 taps per second. (To be fair, that was in my tennis shoes. With the proper dancing footwear, I'm confident I could get that figure up to at least 3.7.) Frankly, I dance like a disillusioned podiatrist with two left feet—and the left one has Paul Bunyan–size bunions.

You get the idea. I'm not known for fancy footwork. The fanciest work my foot ever saw was the surgeon's when I tore my Achilles tendon.

So how's your footwork?

a) **Fancy** Footwork—intricately and skillfully performed

b) **Antsy** Footwork—nervous, apprehensive, or tense

c) **Chancy** Footwork—risky, uncertain

d) **All of the Above** (depending on the situation)

Excuse me, matey…I meant your *faith* footwork. Fancy, Antsy, Chancy, or All of the Above? Before you answer, let's drop anchor in a couple of Bible passages.

First, let's consider the footwork, fancy or not, of our enemy—an opponent who is skilled but can certainly be defeated. In fact, in the biggest fight of his life, he was solidly trounced and left powerless. Yet he keeps getting back up, grabbing his sword in an attempt to bring down another opponent.

The apostle Paul, an inspired faith-swordsman of sorts, reminds us in Ephesians 4:27 not to give the devil a foothold. Let's rethink Paul's words of wisdom in the context of a swords-man's fancy footwork. To do so, we'll return to the blacksmith's shop in Port Royal…but swap out the participants in the swash-buckling swordfight.

Satan, left foot over right, glides easily to his right. You follow with a sidestep in synchronized fashion, your steels continuing to cross. Step by step, you move uniformly. Each blade blocks the swash of the other until Satan lunges forward, causing your sword arm to fall by your side. With that, Satan bids you a glib good-bye—"Ta!"—and triumphantly bounds toward you, tempting you to come over to his side.

You. Me. We've all done the deadly dance with the devil.

On the one hand (or *foot*, if you prefer), we wonder why we keep putting ourselves into the position of swashing swords and fancy footwork with the devil. Paul tells us, "Do not give the devil a foothold" (Ephesians 4:27). Why even let him set foot in the blacksmith-shop door of our lives?

On the other foot (or *hand*, if you prefer), we can't lock ourselves into soundproof, escape-proof rooms all our lives and hope Satan doesn't find a way to slink in. We can't evade the battles. We're veterans of some familiar conflicts:

- battle for our mind
- battle against time
- war of the words
- financial conflict
- battle for our faith
- onslaught of pride
- confrontation with pilfered priorities
- relationship skirmish
- battle of the indulgences

We've walked through the killing fields and witnessed the destruction firsthand.

Lives, hopes, and dreams lay broken all around us. Perhaps if we go into the next battle better prepared, we can keep Satan and his army of fools from gaining a foothold in new territory.

Will Turner spent three hours a day practicing his prowess with the sword. When the enemy set foot in his blacksmith shop, Will met that foe armed and ready. If only we spent three hours a day in faith and obedience to our Father, honing our reaction to temptation. I can't speak for you, but I spend much more time admiring the armor of God—including the sword of the Spirit— than I spend wearing it, practicing in it, and becoming proficient in its use. Paul lays it out for us in Ephesians 6:

> Put on the full armor of God so that you can take your
> stand against the devil's schemes. For our struggle is

not against flesh and blood, but against the rulers, against the authorities, against the powers of this dark world and against the spiritual forces of evil in the heavenly realms.... [Take] the sword of the Spirit, which is the word of God. (vv. 11–12, 17)

We need to consider our footwork when Jesus leads us into battle with Satan and all his covert enticements. But we also need to examine our footwork of faith as we follow in the victorious footsteps of our Savior, who defeated Satan one very holy weekend during a miraculous life-and-death-and-life-again battle.

Simon Peter wrote, "To this you were called, because Christ suffered for you, leaving you an example, that you should follow in his steps" (1 Peter 2:21).

Step by step, in step with our Savior.

We are called to follow in His footsteps. His feet lead us back to those killing fields we witnessed. There, He breathes life into once lifeless bodies. Gracefully He puts lives slashed by sin back together again with His forgiving power and peace.

Christ takes the lead, He sets the pace, and He lays out the course for us as we follow Him. Don't worry, we'll recognize His feet as we follow in His steps—they're the ones scarred by Roman nails.

So, with all that in mind, how's your faith footwork?

Don't Let the Redcoats Get You Down

PIRATES HOOK

Lads and lasses, as Captain Jack tells it, this swashbuck-lin' scene in Ye Ole Blacksmith Shoppe ain't no landcrabs' tale. These two fine duelers make the match worthy of a king's ransom. Swordsman against swordsman, 'tis. Fresh out of uncharted waters comes ye Jack Sp—make that ye Captain *Jack Sparrow.* And defending the honor of the home court, the debonair blacksmith, smooth with ye ol' weapons, Mr. Will Turner.

Hold on to yer plunder, thar's been a development. Ooooh—that had to hurt. Out of the dark, the scurvy dog, Mr. Brown, proprietor of Ye Ole Blacksmith Shoppe, cracks his bottle over the pirate's skull. That Brown feller must be a mean one, mates!

Jack's out with a bumper. He ain't ready for a date with Davy Jones's locker yet, but he was KO'd in round two by the inebriated tag team partner of Will Turner. An unfair duel fer sure, but the redcoats don't care how they capture the charcoal-eyed pirate.

Redcoats storm the joint, surroundin' the knocked-out pirate who lies belly down on the dirt-strewn floor of the blacksmith shop. All bayonets point at his out-to-the-world body as Commodore Norrington drools pride over his treasure trove of a pirate.

Be Captain Jack down fer th' count?

DISCOVERING THE TREASURE

Even though Jack finds himself knocked out and lying facedown on the blacksmith's floor, he doesn't let it get him down. And even though the redcoats lure Jack into the dungeon, their actions don't crush his spirits. He has a healthy appetite for hope, no matter the situation.

Waking up to a world intoxicated with sin brings us shoulder to shoulder with people and situations that can easily bring us down. Too often our life-ship travels take us through waters polluted by negativity, pride, and anger. Dangerous jutting rocks of hate, guilt, and insecurities make the passage difficult. It's so easy to give up, or at the very least, to allow the surroundings to bring us down physically, mentally, emotionally, and even spiritually. The list of discouragers includes:

- vicious lies and vindictive cries
- words that hurt and a world of hurts
- weather forecasts that look dreary and dreary financial forecasts to weather
- spiteful rumors and spiteful humor

- positively bad results on a school test and positive medical test results
- words that intimidate and words that irritate
- insignificant, pointless arguments and argumentative points made by your significant other
- demeaning attitudes and not enough meaningful latitude for the repentant
- overbooked schedules and overlooked responsibilities on our schedule
- ingratitude and ineptitude

Our list of demeaning, depressing, and defeating situations, words, and people could easily be expanded and wrap around the upper deck of the *Black Pearl* several times.

Do we find ourselves down for the count? Do we give up hope? Does faith offer something that brings us to our feet?

As you know, pirates use words and terms not usually found in our vernacular. Case in point—the swash-by-swash commentary on the swordfight in the blacksmith's shop at the beginning of this chapter. The phrase "ain't no landcrabs' tale" in the JSV (Jack Sparrow Version) of this *Pirates* Hook certainly be new t' me.

At times, words and phrases we don't ordinarily use in everyday conversations appear in the Bible. Case in point—one of my favorite biblical treasures, Zephaniah 3:16–17, contains these words:

> "Do not fear, O Zion;
> do not let your hands hang limp.
> The LORD your God is with you,
> he is mighty to save.
> He will take great delight in you,

he will quiet you with his love,
he will rejoice over you with singing."

I'm guessing no one has ever instructed you, "Don't let your hands hang limp." While that phrase isn't a part of our vernacular, it's common in another not-so-foreign language—body language. Zephaniah probably didn't realize he taught body language, but he knew that when we're listless and lethargic, our hands hang limp. When we give up, our hands flop at our sides. Energy gives way to apathy, our hands drop, our shoulders sag, and our backs slouch. Get the picture?

Maybe that's your posture right now. Maybe your shoulders sag dejectedly or in depression because you've given in to temptation. Perhaps you're wringing your hands with worry that God might find it difficult to forgive you, and the person you hurt find it impossible. Maybe an illness or an uncertainty has made you afraid for the future. Maybe your hands hang limp because you face a daunting task you just don't have the strength for. Perhaps you regret leaving your hands hanging limply at your side instead of reaching out to help or embrace another. Zephaniah contrasted the language of our limply hanging hands with the language spoken by the posture of God, whose hands are simultaneously strong and powerful enough to save us, yet gentle and loving enough to lift our shoulders and straighten our backs.

Another prophet, Zechariah, also knew a thing or two about body language. His vernacular was the opposite of Zephaniah's.

"As you have been an object of cursing among the nations, O Judah and Israel, so will I save you, and you will be a blessing. Do not be afraid, but let your hands be strong." (Zechariah 8:13)

Whereas Zechariah emphasizes God as our source of strength, Zephaniah focuses instead on our own human, innate tendency to give up and give in when fear confronts us. God, through Zephaniah, challenges us to change internally. Whereas Zephaniah focuses on our own human, innate tendency to give up and give in when fear confronts us, Zechariah emphasizes God as our source of strength. While Zephaniah challenges us to change internally, Zechariah challenges us to declare/express that change in action.

But how do we change our fearful, dejected hearts? First, we go before God with our hands outstretched, in humility and submission, in prayer. We look to our Creator God as our only source of strength. We ask for a measure of that strength for our hands, our lives, and our faith. We ask Him to change us from the inside out, and we promise to allow him opportunities to do it.

Yes, we allow Him opportunities. We don't just let our hands remain limp. We let God make them strong by:

- surrounding ourselves with His Scripture promises
- spending time with Christian friends who will guide and support us
- concentrating on that which is true, noble, right, pure, lovely, admirable, and praiseworthy, as Paul suggests in Philippians 4:8–9
- focusing our attention on His gifts of joy, grace, and hope
- spending one-on-one time with the Life-Restorer in prayerful dialogue

- investing in encouraging, Christ-centered music, reading, and entertainment
- laughing again…real laughter, not the fake stuff
- allowing the Spirit to rebuild our faith through private or shared worship
- reaching outside ourselves to others
- letting go of the legalism that confines our lives and faith
- embracing God's forgiveness
- realizing we may need to make God-directed life changes

Then, we listen to our Lord, not only when He says, "Do not let your hands hang limp," but also when He says, "Let your hands be strong." The message clearly is to quit looking for potency within ourselves; to look instead to the real source of strength— the nail-scarred hands of the Savior, the all-mighty muscles of the almighty Father, and the strength-sustaining power of the Holy Spirit; and then to allow a change in our hearts, our attitudes, our lives.

In other words, don't let the redcoats of your life get you down; rather, be raised up in the strength of the hero in our story, Jesus Christ.

Notice the change in body language. Our once limp, wimpy hands can now flex with God-muscles. Hands clap! Fists punch the air! Backs straighten! Adrenaline flows! Shoulders broaden! Hands wave! Arms are strong!

While the shouts of victory and power continue, we discover Christ has replaced our human weaknesses with His conquering God-strength. He lifts us up when life gets us down. He declares us strong, and fits us with Christ's own God-strength.

A Child of Royalty Is in High Demand

PIRATES HOOK

The growl of the wind intensifies. The night sky slowly darkens, as if controlled by a universal dimmer switch. There's something in the air. The townsfolk pause, tilting their heads, seeking to identify the feeling enveloping them.

Jack Sparrow catches some shut-eye in his prison cell, waiting calmly for a break-of-dawn date with the gallows. When a recognizable sound blasts nearby, Jack's body instantly goes from relaxation to astonishment. Jumping to his feet, Jack cries, "I know those guns." His eyes bulge. "It's the Pearl.*"*

The Black Pearl *indeed. Evildoers scramble ashore. Pirates ravage the townspeople, chasing the lasses and stirring up fear in children. But Pintel and Ragetti, the dastardly pirate duo, begin a hunt for Elizabeth in the*

Governor's mansion. Like dogs trained to sniff out plunder, the two have caught the scent of the pirate's gold hanging from Elizabeth's royal neck.

Hearing the pirates storm the mansion, Elizabeth's handmaiden warns her, "Miss Swann, they've come to kidnap you! You're the Governor's daughter!"

But is it the daughter of royalty they want, or the medallion she wears around her neck?

DISCOVERING THE TREASURE

Years ago I had an opportunity to observe royalty. Most people stood and cheered, a few heckled, and things eventually turned rowdy. But the Royals were prepared. They assigned a Porter to catch whatever was thrown. At one point, I believe Royal George waved to me! Oh, and you should have seen the diamond—so big I could see it from a long way off. I took in every detail. But reflecting back on the day, I can't help but feel they just wanted to go home—and really, I couldn't blame them.

Twenty-five years later, I remember that experience clearly. It's not every day one gets to see the Royals—unless, of course, you live in Kansas City and enjoy going to baseball games. Did I mention the event I attended was a Royals baseball game? Oops, sorry. Yes, it was *George* Brett who might have waved at me, and Darrell *Porter* was the Royals' catcher. At that time, the Royals fielded a good team and tickets were in demand.

People of royalty will probably always fascinate us. Their presence creates a stir. The paparazzi love them. Their photos sell magazines and newspapers because their lives are so different from ours—and because we're just plain nosy.

Have you ever had an opportunity to meet royalty? Alice did. She lived in a rough area of Washington DC and had recently moved into a new home built by Habitat for Humanity. In 1991, England's Queen Elizabeth II visited Alice's house, accompanied by then First Lady Barbara Bush. Mrs. Bush was showing the Queen how the community worked to build up run-down, crime-saturated areas of DC; the two ladies and their Secret Service entourage had selected Alice's house for a close-up view of the results.

The shocked Alice threw open her arms and wrapped them around the ladies. (She didn't realize the Queen doesn't do hugs, nor that this was a serious breach of royal etiquette.) But Alice didn't stop there. This lovable grandmother proceeded to offer the Queen some of her fried chicken and potato salad.

Alice's second royal hug came on March 12, 2005. At the age of eighty-one, Alice hugged a King. Unable to contain her excitement as she stood face-to-face with royalty, she once again threw protocol to the wind. And who could blame her? Thankfully, the King appreciated her hug and offered an even bigger one in return. He wasn't into man-made rules and regulations. A hug was in order, and neither was shy about sharing one.

Can you imagine the bear hug she gave the King of kings, who saved her and brought her home to Himself? He moved her from a humble, man-made home to a mansion He prepared and built specially for her. Amazingly, this King needed only two pieces of wood and three nails to complete the project with His own hands—hands scarred by two of those nails. From that day forward, Alice would receive royal treatment beyond her wildest dreams.

Aren't you glad we live under the King's grace? That He readily shows His devotion to us, ignoring man-made rules of protocol?

Just think—we have a personal King who…

- loves us with an everlasting love (Jeremiah 31:3)
- takes great delight in us, quiets us with His love, and rejoices over us with singing (Zephaniah 3:17)
- died to save us (Matthew 20:28)
- prepares a place for us in heaven and will return to take us to be with Him (John 14:3)
- clearly shows us the way to heaven (John 3:16, John 14:6, Ephesians 2:8–9)
- rose from the dead so we will live (John 11:23–27, John 14:19, Romans 4:25)
- calls us His friends (John 15:15)
- chose us (John 15:16)
- will never let anything come between us and His love for us (Romans 8:38–39)
- accepts us (Romans 15:7)
- names us heirs of His rich inheritance (Ephesians 1:18)
- forgives us (Colossians 3:13)
- calls us His children (1 John 3:1)
- gives us a royal title (1 Peter 2:9)

Yes, He gives *us* a royal title.
But more than a title, it's an eternal lifestyle.

But you are a chosen people, a royal priesthood, a holy nation, a people belonging to God, that you may declare the praises of him who called you out of darkness into his wonderful light. (1 Peter 2:9)

Do you hear that? Hear that knock on the door to your heart?

The King of kings requests the honor of your presence. As a child of royalty, you're in high demand.

In case you're wondering about proper protocol for responding to such a host—well, I can't be sure about fried chicken and potato salad, but I do know He's more than open to receiving (and giving) hugs.

Just ask Alice.

Honor the Code

PIRATES HOOK

Pintel and his vision-challenged sidekick, Ragetti, continue their dastardly pursuit. The scent of gold leads them to the room where Elizabeth hides.

They call out to her like stray dogs coaxing a lost kitten from a crow's nest: "We'll find you, Poppet. You've got something of ours, and it calls to us."

Elizabeth stands fearfully in a dark closet. She examines the medallion hanging from her neck, taken from Will Turner the first time they met, as children.

Little does the poppet know the medallion around her neck is one of 882 identical pieces needed to reverse the curse on these and other Black Pearl *pirates. The pillaging, pilfering, and plundering crew of the* Black Pearl *has recovered 881 pieces. The last medallion is finally within reach.*

The pirates tiptoe toward Elizabeth's hiding place…closer and closer to the Aztec gold.

Holding the door slightly ajar, Pintel leans against the frame and whispers sinisterly, "'Ello, Poppit!" With that, he throws open the closet door.

Before the mangy duo can say another word, Elizabeth blurts out, "Parley! I invoke the right of parley. According to the code, you have to take me to your captain."

Parley? Parley! What does this royal landlubber know about a pirate's parley? The pirates know they must honor the code, so off they trudge, back to the Black Pearl *and its intimidating pirate crew led by Captain Barbossa.*

When Elizabeth stands before him, the captain turns down her request that they stay clear of Port Royal, telling her, "You must be a pirate for the pirate's code to apply, and you're not. And…the code is more what you'd call guidelines than actual rules."

DISCOVERING THE TREASURE

The movie's reference to honoring the code of conduct caused me to think long and hard about who I honor and upon what I assign value. I realized that I rarely use the word *honor*, even though I do highly respect many people and things…just inconsistently.

Honoring people and things comes less naturally when I want to attach my reverence to God's name (not that I come anywhere close to doing that perfectly). Or maybe *honor* is just not a word we use much today outside the realm of faith. Hmm…

Honor the code.

Honor my God—Father, Son, and Holy Spirit…but not without fail.

Honor my family…but not without fail.

Honor parents and those in authority…but not without fail.

Honor God's Word…but not without fail.

Honor my body as the temple of the Holy Spirit… but not without fail.

Honor moral codes… but not without fail.

Honor Christ's body, His Church… but not without fail.

Honor God's law-code… but not without fail.

Obviously, I fail a lot. Sure, I know I won't be able to perfectly keep that *honor roll* until the roll is called up yonder, but that reminder of my failures doesn't make for the prettiest of pictures. And when it comes to honoring, everything is rolled up in God's law-code.

Honor the code.

A great drama unfolds just before Jesus shares the Parable of the Good Samaritan in Luke 10:25–28.

Setting: Not far from Samaria—around A.D. 32
Wardrobe: Law scholar—robe with bowtie
Characters:
    Narrator
    Law scholar—an expert in Scripture's law-code;
       scholarly type
    Jesus—God's Son, the world's Savior
    Crowd—nonspeaking roles, all reverently seated at
       the feet of Jesus as He teaches

Narrator: On a peaceful day in Judea, milk and honey flowed. Birds tweeted and twittered with joy since they didn't have to sow or reap or store away in barns. Some bored camels attempted to go through the eye of a needle but discovered it wasn't easy. And Jesus' friend

Martha baked raisin bread for her brother, Lazarus. On this particular day, Jesus taught a group of people about kingdom living.

A law expert—a scholarly man—stood up (out of respect for the rabbi Jesus) and asked Him a question.

Law Scholar: Teacher, what must I do to inherit eternal life?

Narrator: (*whispering to audience*) He's testing Jesus. This guy knows Scripture. He's either taking issue with Jesus or trying to find out what He's all about as a teacher.

Jesus: What is written in the Law? How do you read it?

Narrator: This is classic Jesus. He answers questions with questions.

Law Scholar: "Love the Lord your God with all your heart and with all your soul and with all your strength and with all your mind; and love your neighbor as yourself."

Narrator: The man knows the law. His law degree from Shalom State serves him well.

Jesus: You rock, dude.

Narrator: Obviously, the actor is ad-libbing, since the only time Jesus said "You rock" was in reference to Peter.

Jesus: You have answered correctly.

Law Scholar: Thank you! (*High-fives the Pharisee next to him.*) I'll take "The Torah" for $500.

Jesus: I wasn't finished. I was going to tell you to do this and you will live.

Narrator: I guess the law scholar will take "Impossible Tasks" for $100 instead! And you know God's law-code—any man who falls behind is left behind.

The End

Wow! Quite a scenario, eh? If that last statement holds true, we're all dead men (and women) walkin' the plank and telling no tales. No one can keep God's law-code perfectly.

And even if we think we're doing pretty well in keeping most of the law-code, James 2:10 comes along and whacks the reality back in our lives: "For whoever keeps the whole law and yet stumbles at just one point is guilty of breaking all of it."

One little stumble, and we've broken *all* of the law code.

Honor the code? Most definitely. But realize there's only ever been one Man who can and has kept God's law-code perfectly. His name? Jesus Christ. Since we couldn't do it, He did it for us. He accomplished what we couldn't. Remember, any man who falls in line behind Jesus will never be left behind.

What actually took place is this: I tried keeping rules and working my head off to please God, and it didn't work. So I quit being a "law man" so that I could be God's man. Christ's life showed me how, and enabled me to do it. I identified myself completely with him. Indeed, I have been crucified with Christ. My ego is no longer central. It is no longer important that I appear righteous before you or have your good opinion, and I am no longer driven to impress God. Christ lives in me. The life you see me living is not "mine," but it is lived by faith in the Son of God, who loved me and gave himself for me. (Galatians 2:19–20, *The Message*)

Never Fall Short of Long Words

PIRATES HOOK

Despite being surrounded by pirates aboard the Black Pearl, *Elizabeth speaks boldly to Captain Barbossa: "I am here to negotiate the cessation of hostilities against Port Royal."*

Barbossa appears momentarily impressed. "There were a lot of long words in there. We're naught but humble pirates. What is it that you want?"

"I want you to leave and never come back."

When the crew's mocking laughter dies down, Barbossa responds "naught"-so-humbly: "I'm disinclined to acquiesce to your request."

And then he adds, just in case Elizabeth doesn't understand his long words, "Means 'no.'"

DISCOVERING THE TREASURE

One after another they came flying over my head. As a youngster, I was confused. Every once in a while one would come close but still not hit me, its target. The shells made strange noises and were made up of strange combinations of letters. Who would have expected that this intimidating barrage of unwieldy vocabulary could surround me in a church, where people gather to become more intimate with their Savior?

Long words can baffle us, or they can intrigue us. At times the church appears to be a breeding ground for big, baffling, bountiful banalities. (Impressed? I didn't think so.) Even the Bible can catch us off guard with words we don't understand. Sometimes those words describe difficult ideas. Sometimes they aren't a part of our present-day vocabulary. But these challenges aren't all bad. Au contraire! These words often hold a treasure trove of information about our Savior, His work, and the salvation He won for us. Here's a short list of some long words from the Bible that people commonly struggle to understand:

Justification—the act of declaring one *Not guilty*. We were declared justified—not guilty—when Jesus died on the cross. It became ours personally when the Holy Spirit created faith within us.

Sanctification—the act of making holy. When the Holy Spirit created faith within us, He set apart our lives as holy. Every day, the Holy Spirit sanctifies our lives as we grow in God's Word and in love—although our perfection won't come until heaven.

Holy—set apart; like nothing else; in a class by itself.

Grace—undeserved love.

Righteousness—the rightness and innocence before
God which can only happen through faith in Jesus
Christ—not by our own work or merit. God judges
Christ-followers through Christ's perfect life, rather
than our imperfect ones.

Reconciliation—the removal of the barrier between
God and man caused by sin. We are reconciled
with God through our Spirit-created faith grasping
hold of the forgiveness of Jesus Christ.

Redemption—God's act of buying back sinful people
through the life, death, and resurrection of His
Son, Jesus Christ.

And let's not forget the longest name in the Bible:

Maher-Shalal-Hash-Baz—quick to the plunder, swift
to the spoil. Honest! It's the longest biblical
name (Isaiah 8:1). Hmm…quick to the plunder, swift to the spoil. Sounds like our man
Maher-Shalal-Hash-Baz would have gotten along
well with Jack Sparrow and the crew of the
Black Pearl.

Allow me to share one more long word with you—anthropomorphism. In a theological sense, the word *anthropomorphism* means
"to assign human characteristics to God." It's one of the ways that
our God stoops down to communicate with us. It's the way He
whispers into our ears a little divine "baby talk." It's a resource
that God uses in His Word to help us understand Him, His message, His justice, and His grace.

God realizes our understanding of His holy ways is limited. In comes anthropomorphism, the tool our Lord uses when His people aren't getting the message. By invoking anthropomorphism, He gets His message across in human terms. Various passages of Scripture describe God as having a mouth, eyes, hands, and feet. These help our finite minds understand God better. They help us see that we have a God who loves us in an intimate and personal way.

But our God went one giant step further. He didn't just communicate human emotions; He *became* human. In other words, anthropomorphism became incarnation. Jesus is God incarnate—God and man in one.

The Word became flesh and made his dwelling among us. (John 1:14)

Jesus Christ is the Word. God incarnate. Eugene Peterson paints a simple picture of that same verse in *The Message*:

The Word became flesh and blood, and moved into the neighborhood.

Our God deeply desires that we know Him intimately, as best we can with our limited understanding. He wants us to comprehend His words and His world. He longs for us to communicate His amazing Word in understandable ways as we reach out to others. That may mean we have to…

- take time to learn those unfamiliar words and phrases
- explain to others certain church-words and God-words, differentiating between the two

- communicate God's Word clearly, in ways those who don't yet know Jesus Christ can understand
- consider the environment and background of those with whom we communicate God-words
- speak not only with words, but with all that God makes available to us, living and loving under the shadow of His cross, where He communicated His forgiveness to us

But in considering and praying over all these thoughts, we *must* remain faithful to God's Word no matter how or to whom we communicate His life-giving truths. Living, loving, and sharing God with others, we'll hear (in an anthropomorphic way) the Lord singing and rejoicing over his people (Zephaniah 3:17).

And don't worry. When seeking to grow in intimacy with our Savior, we can rest assured that unlike Captain Barbossa, He will never say, "I'm disinclined to acquiesce to your request. (Means 'no.')"

The Best at Times, the Worst at Times

PIRATES HOOK

In the dark dungeon Will grabs a bench and shimmies it under the prison door. After giving it a strong upward push, the bars pop off their hinges and collapse onto the hay-covered floor. The prisoner, Captain Jack Sparrow, has been freed.

Will realizes he can't save Elizabeth from the Black Pearl *without the pirate's knowledge and swashbuckling skills. And so it is, as they travel down the road from the dungeon to the docks, that the men are transformed from adversaries to allies.*

Jack and Will nimbly scale the side of one of the British ships. Though they are two against an entire crew, the duo defeats the odds: They commandeer the vessel and set sail in search of Elizabeth, a hostage aboard the Black Pearl.

From the docks, Commodore Norrington and his redcoat army witness the theft and quickly man the Interceptor—*Britain's fast-moving pride of the waters. Norrington openly mocks Jack's attempt to outsmart him. "That is, without a doubt, the worst pirate I've ever seen."*

Gliding through the waters, the Interceptor *easily catches Jack and Will's sailing vessel. After coming alongside the other ship, the redcoats board the hijacked craft.*

Anticipating that move, Jack and Will sneak across onto the Interceptor *while the Brits search for the duo on the deck of the other ship. Seizing control of the* Interceptor, *Captain Jack Sparrow and Will Turner sail away, leaving the Commodore and his crew of red-faced redcoats behind.*

As he watches Jack sail away, the Commodore shakes his head in stunned disbelief. An officer standing by Norrington remarks, "That has got to be the best pirate I've ever seen."

Commodore Norrington responds grimly, "So it would seem."

DISCOVERING THE TREASURE

His life deserved an R rating due to scenes of extreme violence and obscene language. But his life wasn't a movie. It was reality. As his reputation grew, so did his rank within the group. And why not? He was smart and willing to learn—and having a stomach for cruelty didn't hurt, either. He had no qualms about issuing an unpopular order. Instead, he walked the streets fearlessly, arrogantly sending the opposition to prison. Worst of all, he let others carry out his orders to persecute and kill.

He was the *worst*—deserving of the death sentence.

Instead, he received the *best*—a life sentence.

I'm referring to the apostle Paul, formerly known as Saul.

One minute he was recognized as the worst. He even called himself that—the worst of all sinners. The next minute, people acknowledged him as one of, if not *the* best, most effective missionary/evangelists who ever lived.

So which was Paul—the worst or the best? Why do we do a double-take? Why does our opinion change?

And what about Jack Sparrow? In one moment he's recognized as the worst pirate Norrington has ever seen and in the next the Commodore eats his words, admitting Captain Jack Sparrow may be the best pirate he's ever seen.

What brought about the change? What redeeming qualities did Norrington suddenly find in the scalawag pirate?

Jack's actions changed the Commodore's mind. Jack outsmarted the redcoats and escaped with their fleet's finest ship, proving himself worthy of respect.

And finally, what about me? Funny, when I look at myself I see I'm sitting in a heap of sin. Nothing there worthy of respect. Am I the worst Christian or the best sinner? I can't possibly redeem myself before a perfect God—and neither can you. We'll have to look to the actions of another to see God's redemption plan play itself out.

Paul knew that. God led Paul down the redemption road. His journey, as well as ours, begins with a confession of the enormity of our sinfulness. Paul confesses:

Here is a trustworthy saying that deserves full acceptance: *Christ Jesus came into the world to save sinners— of whom I am the worst.* But for that very reason I was shown mercy so that in me, the worst of sinners, Christ Jesus might display his unlimited patience as an example for those who would believe on him and receive eternal life. Now to the King eternal, immortal, invisible, the only God, be honor and glory for ever and ever. Amen. (1 Timothy 1:15–17, emphasis mine)

While confessing his past sins, Paul also confesses his faith in the Best of the best—the One who changed his life forever: Jesus Christ.

Saul was a homeboy, a Jewish leader born in Tarsus. He was on the fast track to stardom within the Jewish faith. He studied under a highly honored Pharisee, Gamaliel, who trained him in the law of the Jewish fathers (Acts 5:34).

Paul would later tell the early Christians, "I...was just as zealous for God as any of you today" (Acts 22:3). But his zeal was misdirected—until the Lord took hold of his life. Check out the story of God's transformation of Paul's life in Acts 9.

Now try to put yourself in Paul's sandals. It's hard to imagine what kinds of obstacles stand in his way as he shares the saving news about Jesus with the same people he once tried to destroy. What an incredible, miraculous transformation took place in the life, ministry, and focus of Saul/Paul of Tarsus!

You may be experiencing your own miraculous transformation. Perhaps the grace of a heavenly Father who is crazy in love with you is bringing you from worst to best, from worst to first.

We're all in that boat, aren't we? Worst to first...transformed, thanks to Jesus giving us His best.

You've probably heard worst-to-first sports stories or well-known public figures claiming that they are the best in their respective fields. Such arrogance!

On the other hand, I've experienced moments when I felt like the *worst* husband, parent, speaker, writer, pastor, friend, and child of God. And that list doesn't even include professions where I actually *deserve* to be classified "worst"! Because I may just be the world's worst jai alai player, rocket scientist, car mechanic, jockey, or spokesman for weight-loss products. Some days I even feel I could arm-wrestle Paul for the less-than-desirable title of worst sinner...and win.

On the road to Damascus, God opened Paul's eyes to truth when Jesus blinded him (Acts 9:1–16). This happened as Saul/Paul was "still breathing out murderous threats against the Lord's disciples" (Acts 9:1). Paul exhaled vile air, and Jesus breathed new life into him. His transformation from worst to best took place between exhaling hate and inhaling grace.

Christ's life-journey through Paul reaches into my chest, grabs my heart, and gives it a good, resuscitating massage to get my faith blood flowing again. I travel the same road Paul traveled when I look into the face of Jesus Christ. That's where the rubber meets the road—or more appropriately, where the flesh meets the cross. It's where God's amazing grace changes from a hymn to an *It's all about him* lifesong. That's where Jesus turns my 911 into an Acts 9:11, *Always lead me,* Jesus. That's where my Jesus imprinted within a leather-bound Bible jumps off the page and becomes the living, breathing Word who became flesh in order to live with me. That's where my Savior turns my worst into His best.

That's where the Savior turns the worst of us all into His best.

The God-setting-things-right that we read about has become Jesus-setting-things-right for us. And not only for us, but for everyone who believes in him. For there is no difference between us and them in this. Since we've compiled this long and sorry record as sinners...and proved that we are utterly incapable of living the glorious lives God wills for us, God did it for us. Out of sheer generosity he put us in right standing with himself. A pure gift. He got us out of the mess we're in and restored us to where he always wanted us to be. And He did it by means of Jesus Christ. (Romans 3:22–24, *The Message*)

Savvy?

You Can't Accomplish Much All by Your Onesies

PIRATES HOOK

The hull of the Interceptor *moves swiftly through the waters, bound for the isle of Tortuga, its course governed by a crew of two: Captain Jack Sparrow and Will Turner.*

Will sharpens his sword on deck as he plies Jack for information about his father, whose name Will shares. Working the rigging, Jack ignores Will's inquisition... until he has finally had enough. He decides to let Will know the truth about his father.

William "Bootstrap Bill" Turner was a good man, but he was also a pirate and a scalawag who once sailed under Jack's command.

Will stares in disbelief, then defiantly challenges Jack to a duel for blaspheming his father. Rolling his eyes, Jack shoves one of the sails, causing the yard to swing into Will's torso and send him dangling over the water.

Having gained Will's complete attention, Jack now sets him straight. "Now, as long as you're just hanging there, pay attention…you can accept the fact that your father was a pirate and a good man or you can't. But pirate is in your blood, boy, so you'll have to square with that someday. And me…I can let you drown, but I can't bring this ship into Tortuga all by me onesies, savvy?"

DISCOVERING THE TREASURE

I can't bring this ship into Tortuga all by me onesies, savvy?

Captain Jack Sparrow

I am the vine; you are the branches.
If a man remains in me and I in him, he will bear much fruit;
apart from me you can do nothing.

Jesus Christ, John 15:5

He truly believed he could do it—all by his onesies! I knew he couldn't do it. His mom knew he couldn't do it. Even a pirate would have known he couldn't do it. Of course, moms and dads and most pirates are adults. He was a child. He thought like a child. We thought like adults.

Four-year-old Benjamin helped plant the fresh-from-the-nursery apple tree in our backyard. When finished, he phoned his grandparents to tell them about the new addition to the yard.

After explaining all the details, he said, "And now we're going to put apples on it!"

It's fun to explore the world through a child's spyglass-like eyes and peer into the world of the impossible.

Sometimes we try to do things all by our onesies, too proud or perhaps stubborn to ask for help. Other times we know we can't accomplish a task by ourselves and give up before we start. But there's one thing we need to realize, trust, and confess at all times: Apart from Christ we can do nothing. And without a doubt we can't bring our life-ship into the homeport all by our onesies!

What ships are you trying to bring into port by yourself? *The* Captain stands by, ready to take over the helm, as you join His crew.

Lord, I can't bring this hard*ship* into peaceful waters all by me onesies.

> You've heard, of course, of Job's staying power, and you know how God brought it all together for him at the end. That's because God cares, cares right down to the last detail. (James 5:11, *The Message*)

Lord, I can't bring this relation*ship* into faithful waters all by me onesies.

> May the God who gives endurance and encouragement give you a spirit of unity among yourselves as you follow Christ Jesus, so that with one heart and mouth you may glorify the God and Father of our Lord Jesus Christ. (Romans 15:5–6)

Lord, I can't bring this member*ship* into waters of harmony all by me onesies.

> Let's see how inventive we can be in encouraging love and helping out, not avoiding worshiping together as some do but spurring each other on, especially as we see the big Day approaching. (Hebrews 10:24–25, *The Message*)

Lord, I can't bring my citizen*ship* into heaven all by me onesies.

> But our citizenship is in heaven. And we eagerly await a Savior from there, the Lord Jesus Christ, who, by the power that enables him to bring everything under his control, will transform our lowly bodies so that they will be like his glorious body. (Philippians 3:20–21)

Lord, I can't bring this partner*ship* into honorable waters all by me onesies.

> Don't become partners with those who reject God. How can you make a partnership out of right and wrong? That's not partnership; that's war. (2 Corinthians 6:14, *The Message*)

Lord, I can't bring this leader*ship* into waters of integrity all by me onesies.

> We have different gifts, according to the grace given us. If a man's gift is… leadership, let him govern diligently. (Romans 12:6, 8)

Lord, I can't bring this court**ship** into respectable waters all by me onesies.

I made a covenant with my eyes not to look lustfully at a girl. (Job 31:1)

Lord, I can't bring this custodian**ship** into family waters all by me onesies.

Bless my family; keep your eye on them always. You've already as much as said that you would, Master GOD! Oh, may your blessing be on my family permanently! (2 Samuel 7:29, *The Message*)

Lord, I can't bring this steward**ship** into God-directed waters all by me onesies.

And God is able to make all grace abound to you, so that in all things at all times, having all that you need, you will abound in every good work.
You will be made rich in every way so that you can be generous on every occasion, and through us your generosity will result in thanksgiving to God. (2 Corinthians 9:8, 11)

Lord, I can't bring this friend**ship** into trusting waters all by me onesies, savvy?

By yourself you're unprotected. With a friend you can face the worst. Can you round up a third? A three-stranded rope isn't easily snapped. (Ecclesiastes 4:12, *The Message*)

Lord, I can't bring this lord**ship** into faithful waters all by me onesies.

Jesus got [the disciples] together to settle things down. "You've observed how godless rulers throw their weight around," he said, "and when people get a little power how quickly it goes to their heads. It's not going to be that way with you. Whoever wants to be great must become a servant. (Mark 10:42–43, *The Message*)

Lord, I can't bring this sinking **ship** into salvation waters all by me onesies.

I am the way and the truth and the life. No one comes to the Father except through me. (John 14:6)

The waters of our lives are at the same time blessed and filled with ships—hardship, relationship, membership, citizenship, partnership, leadership, courtship, custodianship, stewardship, friendship, and lordship. Some days all these ships sail calm waters and life is good, but on others they roll in gale winds, with one or another challenging us. At times they become imbalanced and we worry about capsizing. The watershed moment comes when we surrender the helm to the Captain and give Him full control as He leads us to the homeport. He'll do it!

I knew He could do it! I knew He would do it! Aren't you glad He did?

Come on, children, let's put away the adult thinking. Grab a tricorn hat, an eye patch, or an apple tree! It's time to set sail . . . and we won't be sailing all by our onesies! We have the Captain's word on it!

Know Your Leverage

PIRATES HOOK

Jack well knows that two pirates—one a novice, the other a well-worn scalawag—can't likely out-duel a shipful of mangy, mucky, mutinous pirates. He needs leverage if he's going to overtake the Black Pearl.

And that leverage is right beneath his braided goatee. Leverage that lives and breathes and answers to the name Will Turner. Here's his line of logic:

1.) *Captain Barbossa and the rest of the cursed crew want Will Turner...or at least, what runs through his veins.*

2.) *Jack Sparrow wants the* Black Pearl *to go with his* Captain *title.*

3.) *Will Turner needs to rescue his beloved Elizabeth.*

But Barbossa has Elizabeth and the Black Pearl.

And Jack has Will Turner and the blood running through his veins.

Aye, Captains! Let the leverage games begin!

DISCOVERING THE TREASURE

Kids know how to leverage quite effectively. They even have leverage tool kits. Pouts. Tears. Whimpers. Sobs. Wails. The kit contains them all. And if needed, the kit also includes emergency temper tantrums that range in size from M to XXL (Maddening to X-tra-X-tra Loud).

Not long ago I heard a thud downstairs, followed by crying.... The situation was serious. That's because the tears came from a little girl, and I was her daddy.

As for the damage, not so serious—just a scraped knee. But three-year-old Sarah felt like her world had been turned upside down!

My wife and I tried all the distraction techniques we knew. We called for Sarah's boo-boo bunny. We tried crying along with her. We held her tight and sang feel-good songs. Our attempts to pacify her only seemed to make the situation worse. What was left?

"Sarah, how about a bandage?"

"Yeeees!" came the reply.

Could it really be that simple? I ran and grabbed one with her favorite cartoon character on it. But as I prepared to place the bandage on her scraped knee, Sarah let out another scream: "Noooooooooo!"

"But I thought you wanted a bandage, Sarah."

"I...[sniffle, sniffle]...do!" She held out her index finger.

"But sweetheart, you hurt your knee, not your finger."

"Whaaaaaaaaaaa!"

Sarah won.

I swiftly wrapped the bandage around her finger and she stopped crying (except for those funny little post-crying gasps which have no name), mysteriously satisfied by her bandaged finger...even while a trickle of blood ran from her knee down her leg. With that single substitutionary act, life returned to its full, happy, normal state.

To this day I'm not sure I'll ever understand that. In fact, I'm thinking of sending this case to be written up in *The New England Journal of Boo-Boos.*

I'll admit, I scratched my head as Sarah walked away...and then God scratched at the door of my heart. He reminded me of all my boo-boos—"sins," he called them. He reminded me of my tears and all the times I tried to justify, hide, and forget those sins. That reminder only made me feel worse. So Jesus took me by the hand and led me to a hill outside Jerusalem, where we stood in the shadow of a cross.

There I cried...cried out to Him. But not all teary eyes seek leverage. Sometimes you get something without trying. You see, I couldn't position myself for leverage, even though He had something I needed desperately.

He said to me, "Surely I took up your infirmities and carried your sorrows.... I was pierced for your transgressions, I was crushed for your iniquities; the punishment that brought you peace was upon Me, and by My wounds you are healed" (see Isaiah 53:4–5).

He won! He swiftly wrapped the forgiveness bandage around my life, and immediately my sins and their scars were removed and forgotten—not hidden behind the bandage, but gone forever. He wiped my tears onto His blood-stained sleeve. Only my little post-forgiveness gasps of thankfulness remained.

To this day I'm not sure I'll ever fully understand grace like that. But God wrote it up in the Book of Life, and so I believe.

With His substitutionary act, my life is now full and happy. I walk forgiven while blood trickles from His life-giving body.

Yes, that Man on the cross has something I need, and He knows it. I try to gain some leverage by offering Him something in exchange for it. I bring lists of things I've done. They don't impress Him. I try making an impact with inspiring spiritual and churchy words, but that only intensifies the pained expression on His face. He obviously has no interest in the leverage game—He prefers reality.

Okay, but I have nothing else to offer. Well, I have my sins, but why would He want *them*? Besides that, I don't really want to go there, for various reasons. They just make me feel guilty. Thinking about my sins leads me to the reality that the cost of my sin is the vicious power grip of death. Even as I play leverage games with the One on the cross, sin plays its own leverage game with me.

I didn't know what to do, so I just stood there for hours. Thinking. Just thinking. My own thoughts and strategies so absorbed me that I didn't realize He no longer hung on the cross. I panicked as I discovered men placing His cloth-wrapped corpse in a bedrock tomb on the side of a hill.

I stood outside that tomb for days. Early one morning it all came together. The one called Jesus—the one who died—stood in front of me. He breathed. He lived. He looked me straight in the eyes. And I picked up on His message. He had won the leverage game! His eyes sang this victory song:

Who got the last word, oh, Death?
Oh, Death, who's afraid of you now?
It was sin that made death so frightening
and law-code guilt that gave sin its leverage,

its destructive power.
But now in a single victorious stroke of Life,
all three—sin, guilt, death—are gone,
the gift of our Master, Jesus Christ. Thank God!
(1 Corinthians 15:55–57, *The Message*)

He had something I needed, all right! But there wasn't a thing I could do or say to obtain it. He just handed me gift after gift—life, forgiveness, guiltlessness, heaven, peace, freedom, hope…and a million other treasures He knew I couldn't live without.

As those gifts continue to give me life, I've come to realize that my daughter, Sarah, has me (and a bandage) wrapped around her little finger. But she knows she doesn't need to use that as leverage in our relationship. And more important, the Man—Jesus—who sang a Sunday victory song has chosen to wrap His death-to-life message around both our lives as He holds us, wipes our tears, and makes everything fine.

I'm still not sure I'll ever fully understand grace like that… yet I gladly accept it.

A Captain Needs a Crew

PIRATES HOOK

A captain needs a crew. Captain Jack Sparrow, specifically, needs a crew to commandeer the Black Pearl, which in days past he captained.

And so Jack enlists Mr. Gibbs, a flask-lovin', down-and-out man of the sea, to pull together a hearty crew for the upcoming voyage.

And what a crew he chooses!

Captain Jack and Will Turner glance down the row of Gibbs's makeshift crew of ragtag sailors gathered on the ship's deck. They struggle to stand at attention. Each seems more unkempt than the last. In fact, this motley group makes The Three Stooges look like royal guards at Westminster Palace.

No doubt about it, this is an odd collection of men.

But at this point, Jack can't be picky. After all, a captain needs a crew.

DISCOVERING THE TREASURE

On June 10, 1930, Captain P. Symons of the SS *Vandyck* set sail for the long journey from Buenos Aires to New York City. His crew included four officers, four engineers, two pursers, one steward, and a surgeon (who charged most passengers seventy-five cents per visit). It also included a barber who charged fifty cents per haircut and offered singeing for those who preferred the quick-burn method to the traditional cut.

My mom, her missionary parents, and her eight siblings (a crew in itself) traveled for months on this trek of over seventeen thousand miles with the captain and his varied crew.

My father-in-law served as a crew member on several ships, as well as under the title of Captain in the Italian Merchant Marines. He toiled alongside hard-working crews of fifty to sixty, unloading and loading cargo at each port. Later he served on a crew of six hundred, on a ship carrying sixteen hundred passengers. A crew that large, serving so many people, had to be first-class, disciplined, and exemplary—in other words, they were the opposite of Captain Jack Sparrow's crew.

Jesus even had a crew—and talk about an assortment of inexperienced ragamuffins! His ship's log lists twelve crew members (Matthew 10:2–4): Simon Peter and his brother Andrew; James, son of Zebedee, and his brother John; Philip, Bartholomew, and Thomas; Matthew, the tax collector; James son of Alphaeus; Thaddaeus, also known as Judas, son of James (not the Judas who betrayed Jesus); Simon the Zealot; and Judas Iscariot, who betrayed Jesus.

Even though we don't have a great deal of information about Jesus' crew, we do know it's a unique group. We also know that Jesus loved spending time with those classified by some as "second-class" and "unlovable."

Glancing at a few of their résumés, we can assume that Peter was outspoken and hard-working, a man whose boat may have boasted an "I'd Rather Be Fishing" bumper sticker. But at least Peter had some experience with a water-faring crew…

Matthew, a Jewish tax collector working under the rule of Rome while cheating his own people out of money, was a social misfit who could have cheated Peter out of money.

And then there was Simon the Zealot. Zealots were Jewish nationalists determined to drive out the Romans using any tactic necessary, even violence. We don't know if Simon was, or had been, a member of a *fanatical* order of zealots, but it seems likely that Matthew and Simon the Zealot were at opposite ends of the political spectrum.

Obviously, this crew needed a Captain or they would sink fast.

Remember Jack Sparrow's face in the movie as he looked down the row at his new crew? Who else would have conceded to taking such a group of misfits on such an important voyage? I'm not comparing Jack's crew of scalawags to Jesus' crew of disciples. Anyway, it's more likely Jack's crew is comparable to Jesus' modern-day crew—us! Just take a look at some of the ways in which we're diverse.

- Some of us have taken right hooks from life; others are hooked on life.
- Some of us are retired; others are just tired.
- Some of us can't speak; others have friends who speak for them.
- Some of us battle addictions; others have addictive personalities.
- Some of us swab the decks; others are decked out with clothes from the swap meet.

- Some of us have mates who pilfered their hearts; others would treasure having a first mate.
- Some of us shiver our timbers; others make us shiver with their *timbre*.
- Some of us struggle to get by; others struggle even to try.
- Some of us daily deal with pain; others daily deal with someone who can be a pain.
- Some of us have a deep-rooted faith; others, a deep-rooted seed of faith.

It doesn't take a Mensa membership to figure out our crew is diverse, undeserving, unique, intelligent, disadvantaged, talented, rebellious, faithful, willing, struggling, and…very much in need of a captain.

But we don't need just any captain. We need *the* Captain—Jesus Christ.

He chose us to join His crew for life. A forgiven life. A full life. A life in heaven beyond this life on earth. A blessed life. A peace-filled life, even when we sail through rough waters. A hope-filled life. A life working in unity with other crew members. A life transformed by our Captain when we get onboard with Him and navigate His course toward the horizon.

So here's what I want you to do, God helping you: Take your everyday, ordinary life—your sleeping, eating, going-to-work, and walking-around life—and place it before God as an offering. Embracing what God does for you is the best thing you can do for him. Don't become so well-adjusted to your culture that you fit into it without even thinking. Instead, fix your attention on God. You'll be changed from the inside out. Readily recognize what he wants from you, and quickly respond to it. Unlike the culture around you, always dragging you down to its level of immaturity, God brings the best out of you, develops well-formed maturity in you.

In this way we are like the various parts of a human body. Each part gets its meaning from the body as a whole, not the other way around. The body we're talking about is Christ's body of chosen people. (Romans 12:1–2, 4–5, *The Message*)

In Jack Sparrow's world, the captain needs a crew.
In Christ's world, the crew needs the Captain.
Welcome aboard!

Don't Stand on Ceremony When Dining with the Captain

PIRATES HOOK

"You'll be dining with the captain."

  The words aren't issued as an invitation; they are an order. Captain Barbossa does leave Elizabeth one option, however: If she chooses not to dine with him, wearing the fancy dress he has provided, she can instead eat with the crew—who won't care what she's wearing.

  In the captain's candlelit dining room, a feast is spread—seafood, fruit, roast pork with all the trimmings. Barbossa, meanwhile, keeps a close eye on Elizabeth. Her back straight and her head held distinctively, the well-trained daughter of a governor daintily eats a small, lady-size piece of meat, chewing it the appropriate thirty-two times. Obviously, the term casual dining is foreign to

Elizabeth, a young girl raised in the most impressive mansion in Port Royal.

The look on Barbossa's face clearly mirrors his thoughts: There's no need to stand on ceremony, nor call to impress.

"You must be hungry," he suggests in an oily tone not unlike that of the serpent in the Garden.

Elizabeth pauses, but only momentarily. Barbossa is giving her permission to forget ceremony, to overlook etiquette? She doesn't need to impress him? Then she will be more than happy to oblige and indulge! She grabs a turkey leg and tears into it like a rabid hyena devouring meat from a carcass.

No ceremony! Not one thought of making a good impression! Propriety forgotten!

DISCOVERING THE TREASURE

Ceremony—that is, flawless manners and proper etiquette—most definitely has its time and place. The key is to be well-mannered, respectful, and proper while still being ourselves. Too often, like Elizabeth, we use company manners to impress. Why do we feel we can't be ourselves? Why exercise etiquette if it means becoming all plastic and fake? Why do we exchange joy for proper protocol?

Jesus said, "I came so they can have real and eternal life, more and better life than they ever dreamed of" (John 10:10, *The Message*). He asks us to be real, living the life He desires for us. Let's gather our fake IDs, our perfect pills, our Martha Stewart costumes, and our well-worn pair of angel wings and exchange them at the Golgotha Trading Store for the real thing—a Christlike, joy-filled life.

As he described in his book *In Search of the Source* (Multnomah Press, 1992), that's what Wycliffe Bible translator Neil W. Anderson did. He discovered that when you're hunting in the New Guinea jungle with the Folopa people, there's no need to stand on ceremony or impress. The barefoot Folopa hunters move quickly along the jungle's leech-infested paths; when they need a rest or food break, they look for a fallen tree hanging between others in the forest, then squat on the tree in a row, like birds on a wire.

Once during their travels Neil found himself exhausted, hungry, and glad for that rest. One of the men suggested he eat something. Relieved, Neil reached into his rucksack and pulled out a big chocolate bar. The Folopa men had never seen chocolate before. As Neil took a bite, all eyes were on him. One native asked how it tasted. "Great," Neil replied. "Would you like some?"

The man broadened his mouth and sucked breath through his teeth, which is the Folopa way of saying, "Yes, please!" Neil broke off a piece for his neighbor. When one of friends asked if it tasted good, he replied, "Brothers, I'm dying of the deliciousness of whatever this is!" (That's how the Folopa people express their feelings when something strikes them very deeply.)

"What's it taste like?" they asked eagerly. He sat quietly for a moment, considering, then looked at the others and said solemnly, "Like pig's liver." The other men hummed with pleasure. Soon everyone was sampling Neil's chocolate.

In the eyes of Folopa people, pig is the best of all the foods, and the liver is the best part of the pig. The man who was "dying of deliciousness" over chocolate had compared it to the *best* of *all foods!*

I love that story. What a wonderful visual—a group of men squatting on a downed tree in the jungle, savoring chocolate for the first time.

If the Holy Spirit created faith in those hunting, squatting, chocolate-eating Folopas so they came to know Jesus as their Savior, won't it be wonderful to join them in heaven at the great feast?

Some of God's faithful will want to sit properly at God's heavenly table to feast, like Elizabeth when she first sat at Captain Barbossa's table. But I think it would be great to hang with the Folopa hunters as Jesus welcomes them to eat with Him. While I'm sure they'll be completely respectful, I don't think the Folopa people from Papua, New Guinea, will stand on ceremony. In fact, I wonder if they'll stand at all! Jesus will likely want them to make themselves at home…so they may go out and squat on a branch.

Then Jesus will take His place on the tree beside them. After a few minutes of visiting, Jesus will hand everyone a *peace*. His peace. God's purest, perfect peace. A heavenly peace far greater than the Folopa people or, for that matter, the people covered in Christ's righteousness from Finland, Fiji, France, Frankfurt, Florence, Florida, Farmington, the Falklands, and every other locale, from A to Z, ever experienced on earth.

All Christ's resurrected saints will receive a *peace*. His peace. And together, all will respond by saying, "Friend and Savior, I'm dying of the deliciousness!"

How ironic. In heaven, where dying is impossible, we can all use the Folopa expression "I'm *dying* of deliciousness" to express that we are touched deeply. Isn't that the way it will be at the wedding banquet of Christ and His bride, the church? (See Revelation 19:7, 22:17.) We'll receive God's perfect, constant, eternal, indescribable peace, and we'll express in worship our thanks and praise to God for His gift which has struck us very deeply. We'll know perfectly what it truly means to taste and see that the LORD is good (Psalm 34:8).

God's gifts of grace can strike us deeply throughout each day. Although we can't grasp his gifts *perfectly* until heaven, Christ's life and love still touch us deeply, and we can respond through worship, gratitude, and changed, more Christlike lives.

Consider His gifts. Then consider a very appropriate response...

Forgiveness.
  Lord, I'm dying of the deliciousness
      because You forgive me.

Love.
      Lord, I'm dying of the deliciousness
          because You love me.

Hope.
          Lord, I'm dying of the deliciousness
              because You bring me hope.

Righteousness.
              Lord, I'm dying of the deliciousness
                  because You made me right
                      before the Father.

Truth.
          Lord, I'm dying of the deliciousness
              because You taught me the truth.

Resurrection.
      Lord, I'm dying of the deliciousness
          because You live for me.

Scripture.
  Lord, I'm dying of the deliciousness
    of Your life-giving Word.

Rest.
  Lord, I'm dying of the deliciousness
    because You bring me deep, true rest.

Worship.
    Lord, I'm dying of the deliciousness
      because Your gifts cause me to respond.

Salvation.
      Lord, I'm dying of the deliciousness
        because You rescued me from hell
          and give me heaven.

Lord, thank You for giving each of us a peace. Your peace.

Lord, hear each of us as we, living in Your presence, hum with pleasure like the Folopa people.

Lord, lead us to others with whom we can share a *peace*. Your peace on earth and Your *perfect* peace saved for us in heaven.

The Greed Creed

PIRATES HOOK

Captain Barbossa dangles the gold medallion before Elizabeth's eyes, then dramatically lays out the details of the sordid story.

"This is Aztec gold. One of 882 identical pieces delivered in a stone chest to Cortez himself. Blood money, paid to stem the slaughter he wreaked upon them with his armies. But the greed of Cortez was insatiable."

Slowly and deliberately, Barbossa unfolds the tale of the pirates' search for Cortez's gold-filled coffer. "Find it, we did. There be the chest. Inside be the gold. And we took them all. We spent them and traded them and frittered them away on drink and food and pleasurable company.

"Compelled by greed we were, but now we are consumed by it."

So it is that Elizabeth learns about the pirate greed creed.

DISCOVERING THE TREASURE

My leg bounced nervously, keeping pace with my heart rate. I wasn't hungry, but I bit my fingernails anyway. I couldn't stop praying. "Lord, forgive me if it is a mistake to do this. I don't believe I've made this decision out of greed, but You know my heart. Is this gambling? If greed or selfishness (or any sin) is my motivation, don't let them choose me. Then I'll know this is not Your will."

Trying to distract myself from my present situation, I recalled attending the game show's tryouts in the great hall of a local hotel. I vaguely remembered receiving the letter postmarked from California informing me that of five hundred who tried out, I had been chosen—along with twenty others—to play The Wheel at NBC's studios in Los Angeles!

Reality interrupted my reminiscence when someone announced that three names remained on the list of players for the final taping that day. If three would play, why were four of us still sitting nervously in the front row of the audience?

The stage manager called out, "Suzanne." A little scream of joy burst from her mouth. Then Kelly heard his name announced, and he ran to take a place behind the big, heavy wheel.

They pulled the last piece of paper, unfolded it, and read the name "Tim."

No scream, just a big exhale of prayer-breath. After hearing my name, I continued to wonder if I'd done the right thing. Even the show's name suggests greed. Meanwhile, the unchosen woman next to me sobbed. She would return to Minnesota with nothing to show for her trip to Southern California but a couple of free meals, a hotel bill, and tearstained cheeks.

Thirty minutes later I found myself standing next to Pat Sajak, while Vanna White posed by the puzzleboard. Pat looked at me and said, "You've won over $14,000 in prizes, and you want more?"

I smiled back and said, "I want more."

Immediately, I couldn't believe I said it.

Stop the tape. I want to give another answer, I thought. But it was too late for that. Millions and millions of people heard me announce to the world that I wanted more.

And for solving the final puzzle, I did receive more. My concern about sounding greedy vanished before Vanna could clap her congratulations. The excitement of the moment got to me.

The problem may sound ridiculous to you, but coming across as greedy on national television bugged me for years afterward. I even thought, *When the show airs around the world, I'll sound greedy in French, German, Spanish, Italian, and dozens of other languages!*

The thing is, I don't like to think of myself as greedy. Sure, I have lots of *things*—way too many, if I'm being honest—but I don't think of myself as greed-based. I prefer to classify my spending habits under the category poor financial stewardship, not greed. (I know, I know—a sin is a sin, and when we break one, we break 'em all. I'm just trying to work through this greed concept in my head.)

Nonetheless, people usually equate greed with materialism. The dictionary sure does. And so does the Bible.

> "You're blessed when you're content with just who you are—no more, no less. That's the moment you find yourselves proud owners of everything that can't be bought." (Matthew 5:5, *The Message*)

"Protect yourself against the least bit of greed. Life is not defined by what you have, even when you have a lot." (Luke 12:15, *The Message*)

Now that I really stop to think about it, I'm sadly aware that greed *has* penetrated my life. If the definition of greed is an excessive desire to acquire or possess more than one needs or deserves, then I do have *excessive* desires.

I have to admit, I'm especially greedy when it comes to:

- being loved
- receiving attention and affirmation
- being liked and accepted

Arrrgh! That wasn't a fun exercise. It was, however, a necessary confession.

Now, if *Wheel of Fortune* had taped in medieval times with the Renaissance sculptor and painter Michelangelo as a contestant, it's doubtful greed would have surfaced. If Pat Sajak, standing before the final puzzleboard, had asked the artist the same question he asked me, I'm guessing he'd have received a very different answer.

"So, Michelangelo, you've already won a lot of prizes and you want more?"

And the genius probably would have responded, "Thou dost not knowest mine heart, Patrick. Mine focus shall not be upon greed or self. If blessed with more winnings, thou shouldst know I shall giveth all to the church—I mightest even giveth it all directly unto thine Papal See."

At that time in history, artists didn't even consider signing their work. They viewed their skills as gifts from God; their creations were meant to draw attention away from themselves and toward their heavenly Father. This showed they weren't greedy, self-gratifying, or desirous of more attention.

Historically, we're a long way from the Renaissance, aren't we? And our actions are far from consistently humble and Christ-glorifying. Too many of us have come to, at least in part, defend and even elevate greed.

That sinful viewpoint doesn't shock the Lord. He witnesses it daily. He also addresses the greed subject quite often in the Bible. In Deuteronomy 7, the Lord, through Moses, speaks as a concerned parent to His easily tempted children.

Paraphrased, the story goes something like this:

All right, kids, your dad has something important to tell you before you move into your new homes in the land He promised you. Here's the scoop: Right now the land is crawling with ites—Hittites, Amorites, Canaanites, Perizzites, Hivites, and Jebusites. Powerful ites prowl the landscape, like pirates lurking in the waters.

These are all mighty *ites* who want to intimidate you. But I will turn them over to you, and you will overpower all of them. Destroy them immediately— as soon as you see the *ites* of their eyes. Have nothing to do with them. Don't spend time with them or marry them. Otherwise, before you know it, you'll be worshiping their gods, which are really no gods at all.

Don't worry about how big their armies are; rather, trust in My promises of help and hope. Don't even think about worshiping their faux-gods. Make sure you destroy the carved gods.

Don't let greed tempt you when you see the idols' silver and gold. Don't take the gold for yourselves. I hate the greediness their gold symbolizes. Preserve My holiness by destroying it and burying it along with any greedy thoughts in your mind.

As the Lord prepared to lead His children into the Promised Land, He told them not to fear the various *ites* in the land. He also warned them about the tempting call of greed that would meet them as they moved into their new land.

He not only warns us about the sin of greed, but He also lovingly reminds us of some other *ites* in our lives...

"You're blessed when you've worked up a good appet*ite* for God. He's food and drink in the best meal you'll ever eat." (Matthew 5:6, *The Message*)

The sacrifices of God are a broken spirit; a broken and contr*ite* heart, O God, you will not despise. (Psalm 51:17)

"Come now, let us reason together," says the LORD. "Though your sins are like scarlet, they shall be as wh*ite* as snow; though they are red as crimson, they shall be like wool." (Isaiah 1:18)

Captain Barbossa confessed to Elizabeth that at one time the pirates were compelled by greed...but now they're consumed by it.

Our confession (of faith) proclaims that we are not only compelled by Christ's saving deed; we're consumed by it.

May that be our creed.

Believe in Ghost Stories— You're in One

PIRATES HOOK

Where has he come from, this ghostly looking Captain Barbossa who paces the dining room and now moves slowly around the chair in which his lovely but unwilling dinner guest sits? Is he straight out of a ghost story?

Barbossa's mesmerizing voice and bulging eyes lure Elizabeth into his ghastly tale of Aztec gold, treasure chests, and curses.

"I don't believe in ghost stories," she replies coldly—yet she is intrigued despite herself.

Her comment amuses the scalawag. He looks her in the eye and says, "You best start believing in ghost stories, Miss Turner. You're in one."

DISCOVERING THE TREASURE

Did you do a double-take when you read the title of this chapter, "Believe in Ghost Stories—You're *in* One"?

Let's face it: Christians get spooked pretty easily by ghost stories—that is, unless we're talking about the *Holy* Ghost.

Ah yes, the Holy Ghost, aka the Holy Spirit. Now we feel better. Or do we?

Even Christians sometimes wriggle uncomfortably in their chairs when the conversation shifts to the Holy Ghost—especially those who came of age in the late 1960s and early '70s, when it seemed somebody pulled anchor on the Holy Ghost and let Him sail the Christian waters freely. It was around this time that the word *charismatic* climbed aboard and raised a red flag. Christians grew nervous. I'm not convinced mainline Christendom knew how to handle the Holy Spirit. And many Christians were quite sure they didn't want the Holy Spirit handling *them*!

Nevertheless, as Christians we can boldly proclaim that we believe in (Holy) Ghost stories because we are in fact *in* one!

Let me clarify that. Anyone who confesses Jesus Christ as Lord is in a (Holy) Ghost story. First Corinthians 12:3 confirms that the Holy Spirit creates faith within us: "No one can say, 'Jesus is Lord,' except by the Holy Spirit."

The Holy Spirit not only creates faith, but also...

- lives within us (1 Corinthians 3:16)
- causes us to bear perfectly ripe fruits of love, joy, peace, patience, kindness, goodness, faithfulness, gentleness, and self-control (Galatians 5:22–23)
- carefully teaches us and leads our feet of faith in the way of God's truth while helping us understand the teachings of our Savior (John 16:12–13)
- prays for us, even shaping perfect prayers out of our sighs and *why's* (Romans 8:26–27, *The Message*)

- gives life and sustains our faith life (John 6:63)
- is a limitless gift from heaven (John 3:34)

You might want to read 1 Corinthians chapter 2. It's a great (Holy) Ghost story that includes this spirited truth: "You've seen and heard it [Jesus' story] because God by his Spirit has brought it all out into the open before you. The Spirit, not content to flit around on the surface, dives into the depths of God, and brings out what God planned all along" (1 Corinthians 2:10, *The Message*).

Do you realize that we can only have faith if the (Holy) Ghost includes us in His story? That we can only continue believing with the Holy Spirit's help? That we can only understand God's Word and know God's will with His guidance? That we can only have a relationship with the One who gives us life through the life-giving Spirit?

How awesome is it that the Spirit chose us to participate in this (Holy) Ghost story?

I find myself surprised and amazed by the Spirit's creativity. And then I find myself surprised that I'm surprised, because God and creativity are practically synonymous. As a former pastor and now a writer and speaker, I love, love, *love* it when I know He directs me, putting phrases together and leading me to Scripture passages that best serve God's purpose. That thrills me to no end.

Sometimes the Spirit's creativity even makes me laugh, like the time a member of our church asked me to officiate at a family member's funeral. (That's not the made-me-laugh part.) Turned out the man who died *loved* to bowl. He was in several bowling leagues and deeply enjoyed spending time at the bowling alley.

I always count on God's Spirit to plant an idea's seed in my mind for personalizing funeral services, thereby bringing Christ the Life Changer into grief-filled lives. As I prepared for this message, I paced my office, trying to figure out how to tie Scripture in with bowling.

I prayed. I paced. I put on bowling shoes and continued to pace and pray.

Aha! I've got it! Thank You, Holy Spirit.

I ran to grab my Bible and opened it to Romans 8. There *was* a bowling reference in the Bible! *Holy Spirit, You are so creative.* I was looking at the perfect Scripture passage for this funeral message.

> What, then, shall we say in response to this? If God is for us, who can be against us? He who did not *spare* his own Son, but gave him up for us all—how will he not also, along with him, graciously give us all things? (Romans 8:31–32, emphasis mine—obviously!)

From there, the ideas started flowing.

When a bowler starts the first frame, he hopes to bowl a perfect game. It's the same for us: We wake up and hope it's going to be a perfect day—that we'll be perfect that entire day. We remember the new start God gives us through His clean-slate forgiveness. We are ready to start fresh.

However, most bowlers eventually miss the mark and have to accept that a perfect game is out of sight. Neither do Christians get far without missing the mark. Sin makes perfection impossible. Repentant, we return to our Savior and start over.

The best a bowler can do after missing the mark is to try for a spare. Fortunately for us, our heavenly Father didn't spare His own Son in helping us make this spare. No, He even wiped Him off the floor…for us! His Son bowled us over with His perfect game. He *had* to, so we could have the gift of heaven.

Ideas continued to shoot from my Spirit-directed thinking like bowling balls from the return machine. Finally, I felt prepared to deliver that message. I'd made it very personal. It clearly contained both law and gospel. Christ's hope for sinners would be proclaimed through His Word.

I arrived at the funeral home to find its chapel with standing room only left. People without seats lined the walls.

Seeing all those people rattled my confidence. Just before the service, I froze. What in the world had I been thinking? I couldn't talk bowling strategy at a funeral! Before me sat a grieving family, and all I had was "for God did not *spare* his own Son but gave him up for us all"?

The service was poised to begin and I had nothing else to go with on the spur of the moment. I prayed, *Please, Lord, don't let them be offended or upset! May Your words bring comfort.*

I began the message by telling them I'd found a bowling reference in the Bible. I shared Romans 8:31–32, emphasizing the word *spare*. Out of the corner of my eye, I warily stole a glance at the mourners. Wow. That passage had obviously scored a strike in their lives. Their grief-glazed expressions had disappeared, and the Holy Ghost was allowing their hearts to hear God's Word. The bowling tie-in was right down their alleys.

I learned later that the chapel was overflowing with the deceased man's bowling buddies—many of whom had never heard that God didn't *spare* His own Son but gave Him up for them. Two days later, the bowling alley's owner stopped by my office to tell me that the message was still being discussed at the bowling alley.

Don't tell me the Holy Spirit doesn't creatively work through us in reaching out to people with the saving gospel of Jesus Christ. I love to witness (Holy) Ghost stories come to life all around me.

I look forward to the day when we can exchange (Holy) Ghost stories at the feet of the Son whose life wasn't spared so He could make sure ours were. We'll be there together—all because Jesus gave His life for us and the Holy Spirit created a saving faith within us.

I can't wait to hear your (Holy) Ghost stories one day. You'll recognize me easily in heaven. I'll be the spirited one wearing a white robe of righteousness and a pair of green, beige, and turquoise bowling shoes.

Sailing Through the Storms

PIRATES HOOK

With a crew of madmen under his command, Captain Jack Sparrow stands proudly on the bridge, one hand on the mariner's wheel and the other holding his compass that doesn't point north. (Since they aren't heading north anyway, that minor detail doesn't really matter.)

But not all is smooth sailing for Jack and his misfit crew. While trying to catch up with the Black Pearl and the treasure ahead of them, they encounter storms. And the storms come with full force. The ship bounces about like a cork on the high seas. Bolts of lightning illuminate the sky as well as the panicked faces of each straining scalawag on deck. They are bounced from port to starboard and back again by the waves overcoming the ship. Yet the Pearl sails on through the storm, until the sailors finally catch sight of their goal at the break of a calm dawn.

DISCOVERING THE TREASURE

As soon as arrangements were complete for our sailing to Italy, Paul and a few other prisoners were placed under the supervision of a centurion named Julius, a member of an elite guard. We boarded a ship bound for Ephesus and ports west. The next day we put in at Sidon. Julius treated Paul most decently—let him get off the ship and enjoy the hospitality of his friends there.

> Haunting storm clouds hover in the western skies. Additional clouds of guilt and fear hang over Jane, who is still reeling from last night's argument with her husband. She climbs into her car and heads out to run a list of errands (not exactly the way she wants to spend her day off). She pulls into the coffee shop parking lot. More important than a pick-me-up cappuccino is the hope of some pick-me-up conversation with the friends who join her at the corner table.

Out to sea again, we sailed north under the protection of the northeast shore of Cyprus, then along the coast westward to the port of Myra. We ran into bad weather and found it impossible to stay on course. After much difficulty, we finally made it to the southern coast of the island of Crete and docked at Good Harbor (appropriate name!).

> Back on the road, the storm clouds begin to roll in and the winds pick up. Jane is just slipping a CD into her car's stereo when the car veers sharply to the right, onto the shoulder. The rhythmic thump tells Jane she is riding on a rim—the back right tire has gone flat. Jane slaps her hands against the steering wheel in frustration and looks out the window as the storm draws closer and closer.

By this point we had lost a lot of time. It would be stormy weather from now on through the winter, too dangerous for sailing. Paul warned, "I see only disaster ahead for cargo and ship—to say nothing of our lives—if we put out to sea now." But it was not the best harbor…a few miles farther on would be more suitable. The centurion set Paul's warning aside and let the ship captain and the ship's owner talk him into trying for the next harbor.

> Little does Jane know that this storm pales in comparison
> to the next storm she will face. Forty-five minutes late for
> her appointment, she waits for the doctor to work her in
> between patients.

When a gentle southerly breeze came up, they weighed anchor, thinking it would be smooth sailing. But they were no sooner out to sea than a gale-force wind, the infamous nor'easter, struck. They lost all control of the ship. It was a cork in the storm.

> The doctor grows concerned after having reviewed the result
> of Jane's sonogram. The cyst has changed in size and appearance, and so the doctor chooses to test the level of CA-125 in
> Jane's blood. Jane's reaction is one of instant panic. The tears
> begin as the questions pour out: *Cancer? Operation? Benign?*
> *Treatment? Chemo? Hair loss?* But Jane's doctor sidesteps concrete answers. *Maybe. Could be. Don't know yet. Possibly.* Jane
> feels herself losing control, like a cork in the storm.

We came under the lee of the small island named Clauda, and managed to get a lifeboat ready and reef the sails. But rocky shoals prevented us from getting close. We only managed to avoid them by throwing out drift anchors.

Family and friends offer words of comfort that sound trite and clichéd to Jane's ears. They are like drifting anchors—not something solid to which she can cling.

Next day, out on the high seas again and badly damaged now by the storm, we dumped the cargo overboard.... Wind and waves were battering us unmercifully, and we lost all hope of rescue.

The dark storms now attack with deafening thunder and lightning: Jane's husband, Mark, unexpectedly finds out he's been laid off his job and delivers the news of his need to seek unemployment benefits.

Paul took his place in our midst and said, "Last night God's angel stood at my side, an angel of this God I serve, saying to me, 'Don't give up, Paul. You're going to stand before Caesar yet—and everyone sailing with you is also going to make it.' So, dear friends, take heart. I believe God will do exactly what he told me. But we're going to shipwreck on some island or other."

Unable to sleep, Jane gathers her Bible and a pile of prayers and takes a seat next to Jesus. He quiets her with His love and comforts her with His hope. Her faith begins to wrap itself in His promises as she sails on through the storm, weathered but safe.

With dawn about to break, Paul called everyone together and proposed breakfast: "This is the fourteenth day we've gone without food. None of us has felt like eating! But I urge you to eat something now. You'll need strength for the rescue ahead. You're going to come out of this without even a scratch!" He broke the bread, gave thanks to God, passed it around, and they all ate heartily.

> At church that Sunday, Jesus nourishes Jane and Mark's hunger for peace in the storm by generously feeding them both with His Word.

At daybreak, no one recognized the land—but then they did notice a bay with a nice beach. They decided to try to run the ship up on the beach. They cut the anchors, loosed the tiller, raised the sail, and ran before the wind toward the beach. But we didn't make it. Still far from shore, we hit a reef and the ship began to break up.

> Jesus reminds Jane and Mark that He has saved them. He promises them that the storm won't be too much for them. Mark dives into the Savior's promises. Jane grabs hold of God's Word with one hand and Christ's presence with the other. They both make it safely to shore.

> Satan wanted them to crash, but Jesus promised to work for their good even in the worst shipwreck. Jane struggled to hold on, but remembered His Word, "If we go through the hard times with him, then we're certainly going to go through the good times with him!" (Romans 8:17, *The Message*).

The centurion, determined to save Paul…gave orders for anyone who could swim to dive in and go for it, and for the rest to grab a plank. Everyone made it to shore safely. (See Acts 27, THE MESSAGE)

Mutiny

PIRATES HOOK

Steering his ship through a strait where hundreds of pirates before him have lost their lives, Jack checks his compass (that doesn't point north) and makes the proper adjustments to the ship's direction.

While Jack plays captain, Will and Gibbs have a little chat about the mysterious pirate with the compass that doesn't point north.

Gibbs relays to Will what little he knows. "Not a lot's known about Jack before he showed up in Tortuga with a mind to go after the treasure of the Isla de Muerta. That was before I met him—back when he was captain of the Black Pearl. *"*

At this revelation, Will spins around, shocked. Obviously, Jack had kept that detail to himself.

Between swigs from his flask, Gibbs continues with the storied background of Captain Jack Sparrow. "Three days out, the first mate comes to him and says everything's an equal share. That should mean the location of the treasure. Jack gives up the bearings. That night there was a mutiny. They marooned Jack on an island and left him to die, but not before he'd gone mad with the heat."

DISCOVERING THE TREASURE

It's the day after Christmas. People's moods have already changed. Everyone feels the post-Christmas letdown. Even the Christmas trees seem a drabber hue of green, and the lights a tad dimmer.

Things change a bit after Christmas—including this chapter. You see, I completed this chapter a couple of days ago, on Christmas Eve. But it didn't feel right. It wasn't what God wanted me to share with you. So I'm starting over.

Because surroundings and events affect my writing, I struggled with this chapter. Christmas and mutiny didn't seem to mesh—until I went to the manger and peeked at the Christ-child. His eyes told me how His birth and the idea of mutiny do indeed mesh.

But it wasn't until today, the day after Christmas, that those two ideas meshed for *me.* Today's events forced our family to look deeply into the eyes of the Christ-child and grapple with the mutiny in our hearts.

Today our son, Benjamin, received a call that one of his good friends at college collapsed and died on Christmas Eve. Leigh-Lane Edwards, a blessing God sent into Benjamin's life soon after his freshman year began, was one of the reasons my wife and I felt so comfortable with our son eleven hours away from home. Thankfully, God provided Benjamin with a wonderful group of Christian friends at college, and Leigh-Lane was a strong link in that circle. How thankful we are also that Leigh-

Lane had a relationship with her Savior who is the Resurrection and the Life. We trust with her God's promise in Romans 8:28 that He will work good for us, Leigh-Lane's many friends and family, from even this event, while at the same time we hurt.

The Garden mutiny. The birth of the Savior. Leigh-Lane's homecoming.

Let's see how one connects with the others.

It's Christmas. I'm sitting at my computer. While Bethlehem is a place of beginnings, my mind carries me today back to *the* beginning.

What a perfect place to begin.

Green.

Lush.

Beautiful.

Perfectly tuned sounds.

Perfectly in tune with God's thoughts.

Perfect.

Period.

The day arrived when God made man out of the dirt of the earth. This is all Scripture shares about this intimate, miraculous, powerful moment:

> The LORD God formed the man from the dust of the ground and breathed into his nostrils the breath of life, and the man became a living being. (Genesis 2:7)

He did the same with the beasts of the field and the birds of the air—formed them from the dirt (Genesis 1:24; 2:19). But things were different for Adam's helpmate. The lone man was put into a God-induced coma while the Lord took a rib from Adam and formed Eve.

With this, God created perfect creatures, the crowning jewels of His creation. Yet some would say He created a pair of mutineers.

Excuse me? Mutineers?

Don't get me wrong. Our perfect God formed them and gave them life with perfection to be perfect. And in a perfect world, things don't change. Or so it would seem.

A devilish scalawag soon led this small crew of two into a history-changing mutiny. The Garden mutiny.

> "You will not surely die," the serpent said to the woman, "For God knows that when you eat of it your eyes will be opened, and you will be like God, knowing good and evil." (Genesis 3:4–5)

Like God, huh? Sounds perfect, Eve said. *I'll bite.*

And that's precisely when all hell broke loose—literally. From that moment on, the crew would never be the same. Almost before Eve could swallow the fruit, she and Adam had to swallow the news that sin had entered their bodies, their minds, and every part of the creation around them.

Sin came loaded down with cargo to be delivered on the doorstep of the world. Everyone entering the world would carry the cargo with them. Cargo of...

- shame and shameful acts
- worry and drive to hurry
- blood, sweat, and tears
- birth pain and pain birthed by bitterness
- broken bones and broken relationships
- the love of money and the lust for more
- depressed, stressed, and repressed emotions

- fears we can't forget and years we'd like to forget
- addictions and family friction
- sadness and madness
- disasters and disastrous plans
- deception and negative perception
- disease and pain that won't ease
- death and death and more death

All of that sin-infested cargo (and a million other pieces not listed) remain as the result of that first mutiny in the Garden. Adam and Eve's rebellion against God has since affected every generation, every nation, every person.

Over the years some of the crew stuck with the Captain, but many abandoned ship, always searching for more, always searching for that Garden-perfect life. But the Captain had a plan from the beginning. He planned to reclaim—redeem—who and what were rightfully His treasure.

Sound familiar?

Climb back on Jack's ship for a moment. Will wants to reclaim his heart's love—Elizabeth. Barbossa and his band of scalawags want to retrieve the last Aztec gold medallion in order to reclaim their human lives. And Jack wants to reclaim his rightful position as captain of the *Black Pearl*. He wants to make things like they were before the mutiny.

Captain Jack Sparrow wants to properly live once again as captain.

Our heavenly Captain will one day reclaim His rightful title—the one not recognized by so many.

Therefore God exalted him to the highest place and gave him the name that is above every name, that at

the name of Jesus every knee should bow, in heaven
and on earth and under the earth, and every tongue
confess that Jesus Christ is Lord, to the glory of God
the Father. (Philippians 2:9–11)

God's plan of redemption and reclamation culminated in
the birth of the world's Savior, Jesus Christ—the Bethlehem
baby, our reason to celebrate Christmas. God graced His mutinous people with the gift of Jesus.

We play the mutiny game—trying to replace God. As the
book of Hosea teaches us, we go around whoring with other
gods (4:12, 9:1, KJV). We think we can run our lives better than
God. Yet even as we mutiny, God offers us forgiveness for our
acts of treason. He responds with an almost unimaginable love
by sending His Son from the perfection of heaven into a neighborhood contaminated with deadly sin.

All this, done to rightfully reclaim and perfectly redeem us.
His Son Jesus lived the sinless life that we can't. He grew and
gave His life as the perfect sacrifice for our sins. He came to actually save us—the very people whose sin led the charge on
heaven's gate, crying, "Mutiny!"

The Garden mutiny. The birth of the Savior. Leigh-Lane's
homecoming.

We celebrate Jesus' birth at Christmas because He came to
forgive our mutinous, sin-laced actions and words of insubordi-
nation, rebellion, and defiance. The mutiny in the Garden of
Eden takes its place in history not only in Eden but also in our
personal chapters of history.

Because of this, the birth of Jesus takes on an entirely different, personal meaning. Obviously, it's more than the com-
mercialism of the world's celebration. It's also more than the

perfectly posed Nativity scenes in homes or on Christmas cards that look like entries in the *Bethlehem Better Stables and Gardens* photo competition.

Jesus is all about reality. He wasn't born into perfection. He was born surrounded by uncomfortable, smelly, hurting conditions. That's why crews of mutiny-bound people celebrate His birth at Christmastime. He came to be born again in…

- burn units and firehouses
- battlefields and veterans halls
- kitchens and family rooms
- hospice centers and cancer wards
- Caribbean islands and captain's quarters
- foster homes and real estate offices
- prison cells and reform centers
- Vacation Bible Schools and teachers' meetings
- employee lunchrooms and Main Street cafes
- smoke-filled bars and the halls of Congress
- five-star hotels and the backseats of taxis
- funeral homes and cemeteries
- wherever you are at this very moment

Two days from now, my son will stand before Leigh-Lane's lifeless body and celebrate her new life. Tears will slide unheeded down the cheeks of her family and friends. Stories will pass between them. Prayers—silent and spoken—will bombard God's throne of grace.

But Leigh-Lane won't be there. She'll already be home when everyone else is at the funeral. In fact, Leigh-Lane is celebrating Christ's birth at home. She knows that's why she's home and is shedding no tears. She received the perfect Christmas present—

the presence of Jesus Christ. Despite being a mutineer and undeserving of heaven, she knew all along that gift was hers. Though she committed many mutinous acts in her short life (as we all have), her Savior declared her not guilty. Her Jesus reminded her that Christmas is celebrated because He came to forgive, reclaim, redeem, and save her as the Holy Spirit created saving faith within her.

At Leigh-Lane's new home in heaven, the celebration of Jesus' life-giving birth will never end. We can only peek into the manger and look into the eyes of Jesus through our eyes of faith. This past Christmas, Leigh-Lane looked up and saw the face of Jesus—and her life changed forever.

We can rejoice in Leigh-Lane's new life and the blessing she was to so many while on earth. She lived, she laughed, she loved with her whole being and faith. But the tears and questions and occasional fits of anger—our mutiny—continue on earth.

Some will attempt another mutiny, feeling the Captain obviously doesn't know what He's doing. But hopefully, most will experience Jesus wiping their tears, holding them closely, and reminding them that He came to earth not only because of Leigh-Lane's need for a Savior, but also their own.

Things will never again be the same for Leigh-Lane's family and friends. But neither will they be the same for Leigh-Lane, the forgiven and saved mutiny-attempting young lady who continues to live because Jesus was born in Bethlehem.

Welcome home, Leigh-Lane.

Save Your Bullet for the Real Enemy

PIRATES HOOK

After the earlier rebellion on the Black Pearl, *the self-appointed commander, Captain Barbossa, abandoned overthrown Captain Jack Sparrow on a desert island. Adhering to some pirate's code of old, however, Barbossa left Jack his gun with a single bullet.*

Of course, he underestimated the drive and determination of the charcoal-eyed captain.

After spending a great deal of time in the island heat, Jack was…well, let's just say he was a mast or two short of a full sail.

Tempted more than once to use his lone bullet, Jack instead wisely saved it for the right time—and the right enemy. Eventually, and despite the odds, he escaped the island—gun, unfired bullet, and all.

DISCOVERING THE TREASURE

Jack got only one shot. So did David.

Sometimes it takes just one.

David, the youngest of four boys, lived in a different world than his brothers. They served in the armed forces, working on the front lines of national homeland security. David served as field supervisor in the family business. God had blessed him with great faith, musical talent, intellect, strength, and good looks.

But the time came for David to remove his supervisor's hat and don the family hat. So, armed with care packages from home, David headed off to visit his brothers. Little did he know that this trip would change his life in an improbable way.

During the time he spent with his brothers, David grew increasingly interested in their current assignment—eliminating a deadly terrorist. David couldn't help but notice the frustration and fear building within his brothers and their team. The task seemed overwhelming to them, the enemy too great to overcome.

The situation began to consume David. He spent time trying to get information from others on the front lines. His brothers started chastising David for fraternizing with homeland security workers. But despite their attempts to thwart his zeal, David continued. He had drive and determination that they simply underestimated.

The more David studied the situation, the more baffled he grew about the lack of response to the terrorist threat. Why couldn't the great minds in the armed services see the obvious?

News of David's intellect spread throughout the ranks—even to the highest office. David's boldness and determination earned him a personal meeting with the top strategists, where he shared his plans with those in charge. In an unprecedented move, the leaders granted David authorization to put his plan into action. David was given access to the best and most advanced equipment…but he chose instead to use unconventional tactics.

Staff in hand, he set his course. He first chose his weapons. Armed and effectively dangerous, David made contact with the one terrorizing his people. He informed the enemy:

> You come against me with sword and spear and javelin, but I come against you in the name of the LORD Almighty, the God of the armies of Israel, whom you have defied. This day the LORD will hand you over to me, and I'll strike you down…and the whole world will know that there is a God in Israel. All those gathered here will know that it is not by sword or spear that the LORD saves; for the battle is the LORD's, and he will give all of you into our hands. (1 Samuel 17:45–47)

With that, David reached into his shepherd's bag, pulled out a smooth baseball-size stone, engaged it in his sling, and hurled it at the giant. Because of David's force (and the Force behind it), the stone embedded itself in Goliath's forehead. The monstrous Philistine fell to the ground, facedown. His lifeless body, almost ten feet tall, now lay at the feet of the conquering shepherd—a lowly supervisor of sheep in his father's field.

Elated by the victory, the Israelite armies overtook the Philistine armies and, just as pirates would do centuries later, pilfered and plundered their homeland.

David took the giant's sword and cut off the head of the terrorist Goliath. The hero handed over the huge hairy head of the hedonistic giant to the Jerusalem heads of state, and then placed the giant's weapons in his own tent.

The people danced and cheered. "David, David, he's our man. If he can't do it, nobody can!" No, wait—that was the chant of the JBA (Jerusalem Basketball Association) cheerleaders. The Israelites cheered, "Saul has slain his thousands, and David his tens of thousands" (1 Samuel 18:7).

Sometimes it takes only one shot.

Although he gathered five smooth baseball-sized stones, David needed only one, because the battle already belonged to the Lord. That the Israelite armies couldn't realize that and storm Goliath and the Philistine army, baffled David. They could have boldly faced the terrorists, relying on God's readily available power. But they chose to tremble in fear, never taking a shot at victory.

Often it's much easier to look impressive on our own without using the God-power which He readily places at our disposal. For forty days the Israelite army stood on one hill and looked over at Goliath and the Philistine armies.

They looked and acted strong, but never used that strength to gain results.

They appeared impressive but didn't impress anyone.

In fact, they shook and even fell down in fear when Goliath roared challenges at them from across the valley.

They had God-power but chose to be powerless.

We can all relate, I'm sure. Following God's will and armed with His strength, perhaps it's time to take a shot at...

- confronting a giant problem facing you
- mending a broken bond with another
- developing a talent you've laid aside

- going on a short-term mission trip
- asking for the promotion
- signing up for a Bible study or small group
- standing up for someone
- speaking the truth in love
- updating and sending out your résumé
- saying "no" more often
- making the appointment you've been putting off

Jack Sparrow saved his one shot for his mortal enemy.

We have God's power at our fingertips when it comes to taking a shot at something we're scared to do.

More important, we face a terrorist named Satan. We have God-given power to fight that terrorist. Don't back down.

Remember, the devil loves to intimidate by puffing himself up to look like a ten-foot-tall scary giant…but he's really nothing more than a powerless wimp with an inferiority complex, playing the neighborhood bully game. He wants us to forget that he's a loser. He lost out to Jesus. The victory over Satan, sin, and ultimately death belongs to Jesus Christ, who gives us victory.

The battle is the Lord's. Remember?

In his 1529 hymn "A Mighty Fortress Is Our God," Martin Luther reminds us:

Tho' devils all the world should fill,
All eager to devour us,
We tremble not, we fear no ill,
They shall not overpow'r us.

This world's prince may still
Scowl fierce as he will

He can harm us none,
He's judged; the deed is done.

One little word can fell him.

One little word: *Jesus.*

One shot is all it took.

One shot at passing a test might bring a bigger paycheck, but it can't buy a free pass into paradise.

One shot by a doctor might save her patient, but it won't save anyone eternally.

One shot by a hunter might feed his family, but it can't satisfy his soul.

One shot at saving our lives forever might seem impossible, but one shot is all Jesus needed.

Sometimes it takes only one.

Never Fear Failin'

PIRATES HOOK

The plan doesn't seem to be working!

Jack, aren't you ready to thrown in the cutlass?

That blasted curse keeps getting in the way of rescuing Elizabeth!

Will, aren't you ready to give up and move on?

Barbossa and his crew of scalawags are just plain disgusting!

Jack, aren't you ready to hang up your tricorn hat and call it a day?

There's only two of you and two dozen of them bony, pilfering pirates!

The odds aren't in your favor, mates! Hang it up while you can.

You can't stop pirates that won't die!

But you can stop before you die!

Give up, Sparrow and Turner, before you fail!

You're neither giving up nor planning to fail, are you, Jack and Will?

Well, then…carry on, mates.

DISCOVERING THE TREASURE

Failure.

What a frightening word.

Take a sip of it. Swish it around a bit. Inhale its aroma. Then spit it out of your mouth.

Failure. What a horrible taste it leaves.

In actuality, the word itself does not frighten so much as the memories connected to failing.

Obviously, no one likes to fail. Therefore, we spend a lot of time—wasted time—fearing failure. Anticipating failure can sometimes cause more problems than actually failing. Fear compounds fear, creating new failures.

A faction of optimists would say we shouldn't fear failing because it's through failure that we learn and grow, making success more attainable the next time around.

That view of failure certainly has merit.

Others encourage us not to fear failing because the fear conjures worry and tension that negatively affects our bodies, minds, and relationships—all the while pilfering our joy.

That view also has merit.

Paul tells us not to fear failing. Even if failure barges into our lives, he reminds us, we can be sure that every detail in our lives of love for God is worked into something good—"and we know that in all things God works for the good of those who love him, who have been called according to his purpose" (Romans 8:28).

Certainly that view has more than a little merit.

Unfortunately, it's too easy to lay aside good, godly guidance and run away—*before* failure knocks on the door.

Sometimes, when failure does leave a gaping hole in life, just giving up seems the most viable option.

But here's the kicker. As Christ followers, we have a Savior who provides answers for *all* our fears of failure and temptations to lose heart. He provides free—not to mention *freeing*—responses to all our fear-laced reasons for losing hope.

We say, "I'm abandoning ship."

He says, "I'll calm your storms."

We say, "I quit."

He says, "I'll quiet you."

We say, "I give up."

He says, "I gave up My life so you don't have to."

We say, "I'm hanging 'em up for good."

He says, "I hung on the cross for your good."

We say, "I don't have the strength to go on."

He says, "I will be your strength."

We say, "I'm throwing in the towel."

He says, "I'm picking it up and washing your feet."

We say, "You've seen the last of me."

He says, "You'll never be out of My sight."

We say, "It's over."

He says, "It's only beginning."

We say, "I can't take it anymore!"

He says, "I can!"

We say, "I'm *not* taking it anymore!"

He says, "I AM!"

We say, "Enough already!"

He says, "I'm already enough for you."

We say, "Uncle!"

He says, "My child!"

We say, "No more!"

He says, "Know more about Me!"

We say, "I've had it!"

He says, "I have you!"

We say, "I want to hold onto my problems."

He says, "Hold onto My cross instead."

We say, "I'm gonna fail."

He says, "My promises never fail."

We say, "I surrender!"

He says, "Yes! Surrender yourself to Me!"

We say, "It's over!"

He says, "It is finished!"

His "It is finished" brings us to a new beginning. Instead of writing us off as failures, He writes us into the script of His salvation story.

Oh, Wooden Eye?

PIRATES HOOK

Ragetti and Pintel—the Laurel and Hardyesque pirate duo—have their eyes on...well, on Ragetti's eye.

The wooden eye has seen its share of sites in its time—whether rolling freely down the deck of a ship or being dislodged when a redcoat whacks Ragetti upside the head.

But Ragetti has a clear vision of future hope.

As Pintel and Ragetti eye the treasure that lies before them, looking forward to their curse being lifted, Pintel reminds his sidekick that when they're rich, Ragetti can buy himself a glass eye that will actually fit.

Considering the luxury of such fortune, Ragetti admits as he rubs his eye, "This one does splinter something terrible."

Pintel scolds ol' Wooden Eye in a motherly tone, "Stop rubbing it!"

DISCOVERING THE TREASURE

I find great joy in creating new angles on words or phrases. Word play. Turning a phrase. So when the two bumbling pirates, Ragetti and Pintel, steal several scenes in the movie playing with the tall, skinny one's wooden eye, the possibility of word fun catches my eye.

Wooden eye. I couldn't help but jump feet first into the word playground before me. Before I knew it, "wooden eye" had morphed into "would'n I?"

Oh, would'n I have fun with *this* phrase!

The more I thought about the words, the more my mind turned to the words of a frustrated apostle Paul, whose comments in Romans 7 easily catch the eye of anyone scanning that particular chapter in the Bible. His words virtually shout: "Oh, would'n I love to stay on course rather than wander aimlessly through the battlefield." Listen to his frustrated voice calling from the words on the page.

> What I don't understand about myself is that I decide one way but then act another, doing things I absolutely despise. So if I can't be trusted to figure out what is best for myself and then do it, it becomes obvious that God's command is necessary.
>
> But I need something more! For if I know the law but still can't keep it, and if the power of sin within me keeps sabotaging my best intentions, I obviously need help! I realize that I don't have what it takes. I can will it, but I can't do it. I decide to do good, but I don't really do it; I decide not to do bad, but then I do it anyway. My decisions, such as they are, don't result in actions.

Something has gone wrong deep within me and gets the better of me every time.

It happens so regularly that it's predictable. The moment I decide to do good, sin is there to trip me up. I truly delight in God's commands, but it's pretty obvious that not all of me joins in that delight. Parts of me covertly rebel, and just when I least expect it, they take charge.

I've tried everything and nothing helps. I'm at the end of my rope. Is there no one who can do anything for me? Isn't that the real question? (Romans 7:15–24, *The Message*)

Can't you hear him? "Oh, would'n I...love to know what's wrong with me!"

I can relate, can't you? So much for playing with words! The world finds it fun to play with our emotions, our minds, our faith. Satan sneaks into our world, hoping to turn more than a phrase. He wants to turn our eyes to his tempting offers.

We try and dodge the cannonballs of temptation, but too often we don't duck soon enough, and we quickly find ourselves reeling from the impact of Satan's incoming ammunition.

We don't want others to see the damage our sins have caused, so we try to hide the evidence. We sit silently, wondering if anyone can relate to our struggle to stop listening to Satan's playful words. Phrases that might turn up in our minds are, "Oh, would'n I love to know I'm not the only one struggling" or "Would'n I love to know help is on the way!"

Help isn't *on* the way; it's here!

Maybe you're thinking, *But you don't know my thoughts. You don't know what goes through my mind day after day. Thoughts like...*

Oh, would'n I love to get that one fired.

Oh, would'n I enjoy sabotaging those plans.

Oh, would'n I look good by making her look bad.

Oh, would'n I hate to have his body (or lack of brains).

Oh, would'n I have fun telling that loser off.

Oh, would'n I have a blast partying with the best of 'em.

Oh, would'n I do just about anything to get that promotion.

Oh, would'n I love breakin' all the rules tonight!

You think God doesn't know those thoughts? You think He wants us to play the martyr—taking Satan's hits as though there's no hope? Forget that! And while you're forgetting that, remember this: Help and hope are here! Jesus already acted on His promise "to set things right in this life of contradictions where I want to serve God with all my heart and mind, but am pulled by the influence of sin to do something totally different" (Romans 7:25, *The Message*).

Instead of playing around, searching for the right words to ask, just lay it on the line. You might be surprised by the answers.

Jesus, You wouldn't care what I do, would You?

Oh, would'n I?

Jesus, You wouldn't send the Holy Spirit to create faith within me, would You?

Oh, would'n I?

Jesus, You wouldn't hate my sin, yet love me, would You?

Oh, would'n I?

Jesus, You wouldn't want me to repent, would You?

Oh, would'n I?

Jesus, You wouldn't forgive my sins, would You?

Oh, would'n I?

Jesus, You wouldn't forgive *all* my sins, would You?

Oh, would'n I?

Jesus, You wouldn't forget my forgiven sins, would You?
Oh, would'n I?

You may think this one named Jesus has quite a way with words. But He doesn't just respond with words. He acts on His Word.

> God knew what he was doing from the very beginning. He decided from the outset to shape the lives of those who love him along the same lines as the life of his Son. The Son stands first in the line of humanity he restored. We see the original and intended shape of our lives there in him. After God made that decision of what his children should be like, he followed it up by calling people by name. After he called them by name, he set them on a solid basis with himself. And then, after getting them established, he stayed with them to the end, gloriously completing what he had begun. (Romans 8:29–30, *The Message*)

Jesus, You wouldn't care about my praise, would You?
Oh, would'n I?
Jesus, You wouldn't keep *all* Your promises, would You?
Oh, would'n I?
Jesus, You wouldn't want me to give thanks in all circumstances, would You?
Oh, would'n I?
Jesus, You wouldn't want to live with me forever, would You?
Oh, would'n I?
Jesus, You wouldn't die for me, would You?
Oh, would'n I?

Jesus, You wouldn't live for me so I can live, would You?
Oh, would'n I?

So, what do you think? With God on our side like this, how can we lose? If God didn't hesitate to put everything on the line for us, embracing our condition and exposing himself to the worst by sending his own Son, is there anything else he wouldn't gladly and freely do for us? And who would dare tangle with God by messing with one of God's chosen? Who would dare even to point a finger? The One who died for us—who was raised to life for us!—is in the presence of God at this very moment sticking up for us. Do you think anyone is going to be able to drive a wedge between us and Christ's love for us? There is no way! Not trouble, not hard times, not hatred, not hunger, not homelessness, not bullying threats, not backstabbing, not even the worst sins listed in Scripture…

None of this fazes us because Jesus loves us. (Romans 8:31–35, 37, *The Message*)

Jesus, You'd do anything for me, wouldn't You?
Yes, I would.

I'm absolutely convinced that nothing—nothing living or dead, angelic or demonic, today or tomorrow, high or low, thinkable or unthinkable—absolutely nothing can get between us and God's love because of the way that Jesus our Master has embraced us. (Romans 8:38–39, *The Message*)

It's Dark in Here!

PIRATES HOOK

Barbossa and his band of undesirable marauders gaze speechless upon the riches—silver and gold—that are strewn about in the cavern. A stream flows in, washing the coins clean and breaking the silence with its trickle.

No lights illuminate the dark passageway—but Captain Jack Sparrow knew about the darkness ahead of time. Wisely, he fashioned a lantern so that he and Will could safely make their way into the belly of the cave, where the treasure chest filled with 881 pieces of Aztec gold takes center stage, surrounded by an array of other pirate booty.

DISCOVERING THE TREASURE

When I was in seminary I took a homiletics (preaching) class under a professor who loved tying famous works of art into sermons.

My classmates and I were finding it difficult to get As on our assignments, and I finally decided that if he wanted art in sermons, he'd get it.

I'm thankful that I no longer possess a copy of that message. I do, however, remember my title: "Chiaroscuro in Light of the Dark Ages." If memory serves, my Scripture basis was Isaiah 9:2:

> The people walking in darkness have seen a great light;
> on those living in the land of the shadow of death a
> light has dawned.

Are you impressed by my knowledge of the art term "chiaroscuro"? Don't be. I wouldn't have the foggiest idea what it meant if I hadn't married an art major named Chiara. Her name means "light," and the word *chiaroscuro* describes the arrangement of light and dark elements in a pictorial work of art.

With that bit of information in mind, read Isaiah 9:2 again. It contains a great light/dark contrast. The gloomy people of God once walked in the darkness of blah-ness. But then a light entered the picture. The hope of a Messiah. A light like no other broke into their dark lives. God's greatest artistic creation—man—was a lesson in chiaroscuro, especially in light of the dark ages (of their lives).

I introduced various pieces of art into my sermon to illustrate the concept of chiaroscuro. And yes, I received an A on that assignment, along with words of praise from the professor.

I may have written that sermon just to please a professor, but I do believe chiaroscuro falls right in line with much of the light and dark imagery found throughout the Bible. Consider this miniscule sampling of chiaroscuro passages:

Even in darkness light dawns for the upright, for the gracious and compassionate and righteous man. (Psalm 112:4)

[Jesus said,] "I have come into the world as a light, so that no one who believes in me should stay in darkness." (John 12:46)

For you were once darkness, but now you are light in the Lord. Live as children of light.(Ephesians 5:8)

But you are a chosen people, a royal priesthood, a holy nation, a people belonging to God, that you may declare the praises of him who called you out of darkness into his wonderful light. (1 Peter 2:9)

When Jesus spoke again to the people, he said, "I am the light of the world. Whoever follows me will never walk in darkness, but will have the light of life." (John 8:12)

Now, I get the idea of the darkness of the sinful world lacking a relationship with Christ. I understand Satan as the prince of a dark world. I comprehend the truth of Jesus as the Light of the world, breaking through the darkness of lives filled with sin, death, and hopelessness. Intellectually and spiritually, I understand the analogy.

But the light-dark contrast, like the Bible's many references to sheep, doesn't touch me personally. I don't hang with sheep on a daily basis, either. For those references to impact my faith in a greater way, I need the Holy Spirit to work through me as I study about sheep and shepherds.

In much the same way, I may not appreciate the full, life-directing impact of the light and darkness analogy. Why? Because my life is lit up!

The sun, moon, and stars light my days and nights. My house has more lightbulbs than electrical outlets. I have a mini book-light for night reading. My refrigerator has a light, and my computer and TV screens glow. Street lights and headlights brighten my night travel. The numbers on my alarm clock light up. And I have a night light in most every room and hallway. (For safety, *not* because I'm scared of the dark. I just want to make that clear, since that's how rumors get started!)

See why I sometimes feel like I'm in the dark when it comes to getting the full impact of the light-dark contrast in the Bible?

One time I did experience complete darkness. The dark couldn't have gotten any darker, in fact. It happened when I was young and my mom took me for a tour of Meramec Caverns. While our tour group stopped in the deep belly of the cave, the tour leader turned off the lights for about ten or fifteen seconds. I'll never forget that darkness.

I remember feeling panicky, wanting the tour guide to flip the switch to bring back the light. Even though I knew I had my fingers safely and firmly wrapped around my mom's arm, I was scared.

I wish I had more experiences like that in my lifetime to help me better appreciate the chiaroscuro in the Bible.

But living in a world of lights, I haven't had many of those experiences. I'll just have to continue to remember and rely on those indelible moments of darkness in the cave, right along with the relief and peace that the return of light brought.

When spiritual truths are placed in that kind of light, I'll begin to cherish the fact that Jesus, the Light of the World, will cause His radiance to shine into my darkest hours with the light of His Word and His presence. Then I can sing with David, "You are my lamp, O LORD; the LORD turns my darkness into light" (2 Samuel 22:29).

I'll let you chew on that thought while I grab my Bible and go do some light reading in the glow of my office night light. After that, maybe I'll write another sermon on chiaroscuro in light of these dark ages.

Or maybe not.

Not All Treasure Is Silver and Gold, Mate

PIRATES HOOK

Jack rows the small boat smoothly as Will, holding a pole with a lantern dangling from it, makes note of his surroundings.

The two are entering the mouth of a cave that—somewhere—has pirate's treasure in it. The pirate duo sense they are nearing the treasure when they spy gold coins and trinkets shimmering at the bottom of the shallow river.

Intrigue. That's the story Will's eyes tell Jack, who continues to row.

Intrigue? More like a flash of greed mixed with obsession—a new emotion for Will, and a pirate's trait for sure. Jack is witnessing Will's true colors, passed on by his scalawag father, begin to show. And he tells him so.

Vehemently denying Jack's claim, Will steps from the boat onto the floor of the cave. Jack follows. The voices of Barbossa and his rowdy crew can be heard in the distance.

Captain Sparrow knows the scalawags have a hostage in their presence. A hostage named Elizabeth, the treasure of Will's heart.

The twosome draws closer, peeking into the cavernous room filled with pirate's treasure. Barbossa, Elizabeth, and the treasure chest filled with Aztec gold medallions are nearly within their sights.

It is then that Jack offers young Will this wise counsel: "Not all treasure is silver and gold, mate."

DISCOVERING THE TREASURE

Jack's advice for Will, who is discovering that greedy pirate blood runs through his veins after all, serves as a reminder that golden opportunities aren't always wrapped in gold.

Coming from pirate Jack, the words seems uncharacteristic. *The lady, Will. Elizabeth!* Hint, hint. Nudge, nudge. *Know what I mean, matey?* Material things are fine, but life offers more important things, too.

More important things. Like what? Hmmm…like relationships?

Relationships are everything to us, aren't they? Everything we do is relational. We treasure relationships to people and things on different levels, with people hopefully on top. And the relationship God has with us—and we have with Him—affects every one of those relationships.

Matthew 6:21 puts our treasured relationships in perspective…

For where your treasure is, there your heart will be also.

That same verse in *The Message* adds another dimension to the truth of Christ's words.

It's obvious, isn't it? The place where your treasure is, is the place you will most want to be, and end up being. (Matthew 6:21, *The Message*)

I can justify certain *treasures* by saying my heart really isn't in them, so everything's cool. I'm not missing the mark on that one. But when I begin to think about a treasure as the place I most want to be, and wind up going there…well, that's another story. That casts things in a different light—one that shines into the darkest corners of my heart.

I'll come clean. While I have lots of those places I sinfully end up going, I'll share one with you from my life in the early 1980s. I'm talking about my place in front of the TV. I'm not there at this point in my life, thankfully, but in my late teens and early twenties I treasured the television—as perhaps did many of you.

Because in so many homes the television had become the family altar, several family-focused groups encouraged people to abandon their television sets and replace them with family time.

There's actually a Turn Off Your Television week in April. Could people really survive without television? I even read about an entire town going without TV for one whole month!

An entire month without TV? Get outta here!

I admit it—I'm a product of the TV generation.

Like I said, I used to spend too much time in front of my silver and gold TV. Today I can't tell you much about primetime shows. I'm glad things have changed. But let me tell you a little bit about treasuring TV too much...

My blender is hooked up to cable. I named my gerbils Nielson and Arbitron. I eat my supper on a satellite dish. I grew up doing the *TV Guide* crossword in pen!

You think you can be in control without your remote control? You think it's easy putting your horizontal on hold for a month? You wouldn't be a sport about doing without your sports, would you?

After several boxes of tissues and even more hours of staring at a blank screen, I decided that if Michael Landon and the people of Walnut Grove could do without television, so could I.

Initially, I missed EPSN, *The O.C.,* HBO, JAG, ABC, *M*A*S*H,* CBS, *ER,* NBC, and *CSI.* My neighbor started to bear an uncanny resemblance to Kramer. My travel agent, wanting to help, booked me on a three-hour cruise with my sister, Mary Ann, and her movie-star friend. Unfortunately, the ship took ground on the shore of an uncharted desert isle, from which I was promptly voted off.

Listening to the radio didn't take my mind off my networkless nightmare. WKRP in Cincinnati was hosting an *American Idol* marathon. My life needed an extreme makeover. Then the fear factor took over. I was married, with children—once a family guy—and my wife soon felt lost, becoming a desperate housewife. I called my three children Greg, Peter, Bobby, Marcia, Jan, and Cindy. My big brother voted me out of the family. Living like a monk, I ended up going to bed in the middle of primetime and dreamed of hanging a fifty-two-inch HDTV plasma TV over the fireplace.

The next morning, while still mourning my loss, I realized I couldn't get my *Good Morning America* fix, so I ran to an open-early-in-the-morning electronics store and welcomed a new TV into my life, thereby turning my morning mourning into joy.

Tubeotomites live with the hope and faith that their new TV-free family will be a home improvement. Experts say the absence of TV will cause families to grow closer. Kids will start to say, "Mom, Dad, I'm mad about you." Instead of watching *The Amazing Race*, families will enjoy an amazing race into the family room for happy days with a full house. Relatives will play games, talk, cook out with the neighbors, and read...just like the Waltons.

But be forewarned. The participants on *Survivor* seemed content without TV living in the wild, but look what happened to most of them—they were voted off the island!

Okay, that was a bit over the top. Fun, but over the top! But maybe it's appropriate that we all come clean and unearth some of our false treasures. We can all use some treasured time to sit across from the Light of the world and let Him shine into the dark corners of our hearts. In fact, He'll discover I love a lot of other silver and gold treasures.

Yes, Lord, it's obvious. The place where our treasure is, is the place we will most want to be...and end up being.

We really, truly desire that You, our Savior and Friend, are our treasure. Forgive us, Savior. And thank You, Lord, for making us Your treasure. That's what motivates us to treasure You. So come and clean house. We know You won't just rearrange the gold and silver furniture of our homes and lives. You come to transform. You come to execute the extreme life makeover we desperately need.

Jack Sparrow's right—not all treasure is silver and gold.

Know Whose Blood You Need

PIRATES HOOK

Barbossa stands gallantly atop the mound within the torch-lit cavern, surrounded by his band of ruthless pirates and assorted booty from pilfering days gone by. Before him sits the treasure chest filled with 881 Aztec gold medallions. To his left stands a frightened Elizabeth, who has medallion number 882 hanging from her neck.

The despicable Captain pumps up his fellow rogues with a stirring speech. The room is filled with expectation that the ancient curse against them will soon vanish, that their bodies and lives will be reclaimed with the final medallion and blood from a pirate's offspring.

The chanting voices echo off the cavern walls, growing louder and louder.

Barbossa snatches the medallion from Elizabeth's neck, placing it in her open hand. The blade of his sword moves swiftly across Elizabeth's palm, drawing blood. Barbossa turns her hand over the treasure of gold, squeezing it tightly so her blood will drip onto the medallion.

The bloodied piece drops into the treasure chest. The cavernous room grows silent in anticipation of pirate bodies being transformed from ghostly to fleshly state.

Nothing. No change. The curse continues.

Turns out Elizabeth wasn't a blood relative of Bootstrap Turner after all. She lied.

But Jack knows whose blood they need.

Will. Will Turner. The son of Bootstrap Turner.

Now you know, too.

DISCOVERING THE TREASURE

Know whose blood you need.

Those words could have been the subtitle for *Pirates of the Caribbean: The Curse of the Black Pearl.* The movie's plot centers around the quest for one pirate's medallion and one man's blood—but not just any man's blood. The only hope for the pirates' freedom from the curse hangs on their acquiring blood from William Bootstraps Turner or one of his blood relatives. The son's blood mixed with the 882 identical pieces of gold will assure the scalawags of real life.

A blood theme runs through the Bible, too—from Genesis to Revelation. The New International Version mentions the word *blood* 356 times.

I know, blood's not a comfortable topic to discuss. It goes along with emergencies, bandages, hospitals, fainting, scars, pain, wounds, gashes, needles, transfusions, gore, and sometimes even death.

But the people in the Bible's region and time period considered blood an important part of life. In fact, blood and life were directly connected. Lifeblood. Whether we're comfortable with the concept or not, blood and God's salvation history go hand in hand.

In the beginning, blood flowed through the bodies of the animals God created. And when God formed Adam out of the dirt of the ground and breathed life into him, blood also flowed through his body. Adam may not have even realized it. While in the perfection of Eden he never saw blood. He didn't scrape his knees running through the garden. Paper cuts? Obviously not. (Not even a fig leaf cut). Blood loss from the thorns of roses? Pain and perfection don't mix. Surgery, animal bites, and your common household boo-boos were all things of the future.

But things would change once sin came barging into the world. When Adam first gashed his finger on a sharp root while working the fields, he must have been confused by the red stuff oozing from his hand. Eve must have wondered about her occasional mysterious flow of blood. With sin came the knowledge of blood and the necessity of this lifeblood within humans and animals.

In those days and in that part of the world, animal sacrifices occurred regularly. Blood ran freely from altars. The people probably grew immune to the scent of it. The creating and living God sought appeasement for man's sins and their results through the pouring out of lifeblood through sacrifices. You can check out more bloody details throughout the Old Testament (blood talk flows particularly heavily in the book of Leviticus).

Exodus 12 tells the story of and gives instructions concerning the Lord's Passover. God's people, enslaved in Egypt, were to take a young male lamb without any blemishes and, at a time set apart by God, slaughter it. His people were then to take some of the lamb's blood and put it on the sides and top of their houses' doorframes before roasting and eating the lamb. That night God would strike down the firstborn of both the Egyptians and their livestock. But He would "pass over" the homes of those with the lamb's blood on their doors.

God's children were saved by the blood of the lamb. Thankfully, they knew whose blood they needed for life.

All the sacrifices and other blood talk in the Old Testament points directly to One who shed His blood for the salvation of the world...Jesus Christ. The Passover Lamb. The Lamb of God who would take away the sins of the world. The perfect sacrifice for the sins of the world. (See John 1:29, 36; 1 Corinthians 5:7; 1 John 2:2.)

Jesus lovingly went to the cross—despite its shame and pain—to become the sacrifice before God the Father for *our* sins, and ultimately to overcome our death. All the past sacrifices and all the blood that God's people once offered up for their sins couldn't fully appease God. It took the lifeblood of a young male, the unblemished (sinless) Lamb of God, to once and for all take away the sins of the world as a perfect sacrifice.

Through Adam's blood came sin and death, and they passed down through every generation. But through the shedding of Christ's blood on Calvary's cross, forgiveness and eternal life came as heaven's gifts—available to all who place their faith in the Lamb of God, Jesus Christ.

Even the book of Revelation, where we get a glimpse of heaven, leaves us with talk of blood.

To him who loves us and has freed us from our sins by his blood, and has made us to be a kingdom and priests to serve his God and Father—to him be glory and power for ever and ever! Amen. (Revelation 1:5–6)

And he said, "These are they who have come out of the great tribulation; they have washed their robes and made them white in the blood of the Lamb. (Revelation 7:14)

For Barbossa's pirates, knowing whose blood they needed wasn't enough to give them real life. They also needed the last of the 882 identical medallions.

The Bible teaches that unlike those medallions we are not identical. We have each been created unique with various gifts and talents, appearances, and lives.

But we *are* all alike in that we sin. And because we live under the curse of sin, all the gold or silver in the world won't pay for our sins or buy us a place in heaven. That gift comes only through the blood sacrifice and the resurrection of our Savior. Once for all.

Since we've compiled this long and sorry record as sinners (both us and them[those before us and we ourselves]) and proved that we are utterly incapable of living the glorious lives God wills for us, God did it for us. Out of sheer generosity he put us in right standing with himself. A pure gift. He got us out of the mess we're in and restored us to where he always wanted us to be. And he did it by means of Jesus Christ.

God sacrificed Jesus on the altar of the world to clear that world of sin. Having faith in him sets us in the clear. God decided on this course of action in full view of the public—to set the world in the clear with himself through the sacrifice of Jesus, finally taking care of the sins he had so patiently endured. (Romans 3:23–25, *The Message*)

Now you know whose blood you need.

Trust the Anchor

PIRATES HOOK

The Interceptor *glides briskly through the ocean waves with the* Black Pearl *gaining on it. The chase is on. Barbossa knows who and what he wants—the gold medallion, Will Turner, and his blood, all of which escaped the pirates' cavern.*

With its nemesis the Black Pearl *closing in, Gibbs barks orders to lighten the* Interceptor*'s load, allowing it to move faster. Cannonballs, kegs, and crates are dumped unceremoniously into the Caribbean waters.*

Barbossa and his crew ready their cannons and run out the sweeps, using all their power to come alongside the Interceptor*. With the ships close to sailing side by side, Elizabeth throws out a plan to catch the* Pearl *by surprise. The orders go out to lower the anchor on the starboard side.*

Trusting the anchor to latch onto an immovable foundation along the ocean floor, the crew braces for the Interceptor *to turn 180 degrees against the roaring waves. The anchor holds, and the ships sail past one another in opposite directions.*

The chase has become an all-out battle at sea.

DISCOVERING THE TREASURE

It's easy to listen to or read about God's promises. So why do we make it so difficult to actually *trust* God's promises that would anchor us in hope through Jesus Christ?

A boater who drops an anchor over the side can't actually see what the anchor secures itself on. He or she simply trusts the anchor, even when it's out of sight.

In the same way, while we may not actually *see* our divine Anchor in the middle of our deep waters, we can be sure He makes us secure. God does not and cannot lie (Titus 1:1–3; Hebrews 6:18). Our faith can fully trust His promises with hope.

Pray that the Holy Spirit will help you sink your faith in the immovable anchor of hope through our Captain's promises, as you take hold of the truths found on the following pages.

Because God wanted to make the unchanging nature of his purpose very clear to the heirs of what was promised, he confirmed it with an oath. God did this so that, by two unchangeable things in *which it is impossible for God to lie,* we who have fled to take hold of the hope offered to us may be greatly encouraged. *We have this hope as an anchor for the soul, firm and secure.* It enters the inner sanctuary behind the curtain, where Jesus, who went before us, has entered on our behalf. (Hebrews 6:17–20, emphasis mine)

We have this hope as an anchor for our salvation...

For God so loved the world that he gave his one and only Son, that whoever believes in him shall not perish but have eternal life. (John 3:16)

Jesus answered, "I am the way and the truth and the life. No one comes to the Father except through me. (John 14:6)

For it is by grace you have been saved, through faith—and this not from yourselves, it is the gift of God—not by works, so that no one can boast. (Ephesians 2:8–9)

I will not leave you as orphans; I will come to you. (John 14:18)

We have this hope as an anchor for our daily life...

What, then, shall we say in response to this? If God is for us, who can be against us? Who shall separate us from the love of Christ? Shall trouble or hardship or persecution or famine or nakedness or danger or sword? No, in all these things we are more than conquerors through him who loved us. For I am convinced that neither death nor life, neither angels nor demons, neither the present nor the future, nor any powers, neither height nor depth, nor anything else in all creation, will be able to separate us from the love of God that is in Christ Jesus our Lord. (Romans 8:31, 35, 37–39)

If you grasp and cling to life on your terms, you'll lose it, but if you let that life go, you'll get life on God's terms. (Luke 17:33, *The Message*)

Are you tired? Worn out? Burned out on religion? Come to me. Get away with me and you'll recover your life. I'll show you how to take a real rest. Walk with me and work with me—watch how I do it. Learn the unforced rhythms of grace. I won't lay anything heavy or ill-fitting on you. Keep company with me and you'll learn to live freely and lightly. (Matthew 11:28–30, *The Message*)

We have this hope as an anchor when storms arise...

Don't be afraid, I've redeemed you. I've called your name. You're mine. When you're in over your head, I'll be there with you. When you're in rough waters, you will not go down. When you're between a rock and a hard place, it won't be a dead end—Because I am GOD, your personal God.... (Isaiah 43:1–3, *The Message*)

Jesus said to her, "I am the resurrection and the life. He who believes in me will live, even though he dies; and whoever lives and believes in me will never die. (John 11:25–26)

We have this hope as an anchor when we fail...

If we claim to be without sin, we deceive ourselves and the truth is not in us. If we confess our sins, he is faithful and just and will forgive us our sins and purify us from all unrighteousness. (1 John 1:8–9)

And we know that in all things God works for the good of those who love him, who have been called according to his purpose. (Romans 8:28)

For I will forgive their wickedness and will remember their sins no more. (Hebrews 8:12)

We have this hope as an anchor when we pray…

Don't bargain with God. Be direct. Ask for what you need. This isn't a cat-and-mouse, hide-and-seek game we're in. (Matthew 7:7–8, *The Message*)

Meanwhile, the moment we get tired in the waiting, God's Spirit is right alongside helping us along. If we don't know how or what to pray, it doesn't matter. He does our praying in and for us, making prayer out of our wordless sighs, our aching groans. He knows us far better than we know ourselves, knows our pregnant condition, and keeps us present before God. (Romans 8:26–27, *The Message*)

Don't fret or worry. Instead of worrying, pray. Let petitions and praises shape your worries into prayers, letting God know your concerns. Before you know it, a sense of God's wholeness, everything coming together for good, will come and settle you down. It's wonderful what happens when Christ displaces worry at the center of your life. (Philippians 4:6–7, *The Message*)

We have this hope as an anchor as we explore for treasures in His Word…

Jesus did many other miraculous signs in the presence of his disciples, which are not recorded in this book. But these are written that you may believe that Jesus is the Christ, the Son of God, and that by believing you may have life in his name. (John 20:30–31)

I am not ashamed of the gospel, because it is the power of God for the salvation of everyone who believes: first for the Jew, then for the Gentile. (Romans 1:16)

All Scripture is God-breathed and is useful for teaching, rebuking, correcting and training in righteousness, so that the man of God may be thoroughly equipped for every good work. (2 Timothy 3:16–17)

We have this hope as an anchor for the soul, firm and secure...

When God wanted to guarantee his promises, he gave his word, a rock-solid guarantee—God can't break his word. And because his word cannot change, the promise is likewise unchangeable.

We who have run for our very lives to God have every reason to grab the promised hope with both hands and never let go. It's an unbreakable spiritual lifeline, reaching past all appearances right to the very presence of God where Jesus, running on ahead of us, has taken up his permanent post as high priest for us. (Hebrews 6:17–20, *The Message*)

Trust the Anchor.

Anything Is Possible

(Even When Stranded on a Deserted Island...Twice)

PIRATES HOOK

Jack Sparrow's first island adventure followed the mutiny of his crew aboard the Black Pearl. *The way Jack tells it, he escaped desertion by making a raft by tying sea turtles together with human hair...off his back!*

This time the island is reserved for two: Jack and Elizabeth. Barbossa and his band of pirate thugs are holding Will and the medallion hostage. They have no need for Jack or the Governor's daughter, and so they make them walk the plank near the same island Jack once resided on temporarily.

The truth about Jack's so-called miraculous first escape comes out when he opens up to the only other person on the isle, Elizabeth. "Last time the rumrunners used this island as a cache, and when they came by, I was able to barter passage off."

Understanding dawns on Elizabeth, and her mind quickly finds a way to benefit from the rumrunners' left-behind stash. Later, exactly as she planned it, Jack passes out for the night after imbibing in the stash. Elizabeth builds a fire with flames leaping over a thousand feet high to signal the Royal Navy, who are out searching for her. The fiery young lady's plan works, and within hours Commodore Norrington's ship spots the fire and the duo is rescued.

DISCOVERING THE TREASURE

TV and movie directors can make the impossible look possible with their outlandish budgets and unlimited resources. We've all shaken our heads in disbelief over some impossible stunt we've seen on-screen, marveling at the creative genius behind it.

Yet even though we live in a world with seemingly endless possibilities, we still occasionally witness something that makes us do a double-take.

My brother Ted recently told me an extraordinary fact about the mating ritual of some spider he had been reading about. (I should clarify that even though Ted is a biologist, he and I don't usually spend time discussing the mating practices of spiders.) Anyway, the male of this species prepares nuptial gifts to bring his mate—for instance, a bug or fly. Then Mr. Spider binds it up in silk, just like a wee gift. The romantic male then presents the gift to his lady when he comes to mate. The female unwraps the gift and begins to eat it. While the female is focused on devouring the gift, she doesn't notice that Mr. Right is focusing on something else.

Tricky little guy, huh? How amazing to think that a spider would wrap a present for his eight-legged bride!

Creative! Mind-boggling! Deserving of our praise! Perfect! These words describe our God. We can't even fathom all the amazing ways He works within the bodies, minds, and lives of His creation. We could all share stories of seemingly impossible feats that God has made possible.

You may have read about the wilderness man who dressed in camel's hair and lived off locusts and honey (Matthew 3).

Or what about that extraordinary man who, after experiencing the death of his ten children and their spouses and losing all his crops and animals as well, refused to get angry at God? Instead he said, "The LORD gave and the LORD has taken away; may the name of the LORD be praised" (Job 1:21).

And surely you've heard something about the teenage girl who found herself pregnant without ever having been intimate with a man. The amazing story continues with an angel talking to her and the girl responding in faith and trust. The angel told her, "The Holy Spirit will come upon you, and the power of the Most High will overshadow you. So the holy one to be born will be called the Son of God. Even Elizabeth your relative is going to have a child in her old age, and she who was said to be barren is in her sixth month. For nothing is impossible with God" (Luke 1:35–37).

The girl responded, "I am the Lord's servant. May it be to me as you have said" (Luke 1:38).

Nothing is impossible with God.

It's easy to look at some people whose lives are depicted in the Bible and picture them as much greater than us. They seem so…perfect. Consider John the Baptist, who seemed to find following God's life plan for him so simple. He grew up and became strong in spirit and lived in the desert until he appeared publicly. He knew exactly what to say to people. Okay, so his wardrobe and diet weren't so great, but otherwise he seems so...so...perfect!

Job's strong statement of faith after his world crashed appears too impossible to come from a regular ol' human being. He *had* to be bitter.

Mary the teenager displayed the heart of a seasoned faith warrior. She fully trusted God's plan. Astonishing!

The list of examples goes on and on. The thing that we have to remember as we look at the lives of biblical people is that all except Jesus Christ were sinful human beings, just like you and me. We—just like they—kneel before the manger throne or at the cross of Christ or at His heavenly throne humbled and humiliated by our sins. We deserve nothing, while God forgives us and gives us purpose. He wants to use us in the same way He used John the Baptist, the apostles, or the Old Testament patriarchs. Our Lord desires that we trust Him like Mary did, that we have faith to go out on a limb for Him!

As I said, we are all sinful. So why do we expect so much of believers in Bible times and so little of ourselves? Why do we expect so much from the God they worshiped, forgetting the same Lord is in love with us? The very same Spirit that created and strengthened the faith of people in the Bible empowers us. The very same God who called them to follow and obey calls us. The very same Savior who saved them from the power of sin, death, and hell has rescued us. God dwells in us, just as He did in them. God used them and uses us. He gave their lives a heavenly flavor and He does the same for us.

Nothing is impossible with God.

Nothing. Nil. Zero. Nada.

Even if your name isn't John, Job, or Mary, nothing is impossible for you with God's help. Are you ready to make that your mantra?

God makes possible what the world writes off as unattainable. And nothing is impossible with God.

Did I already mention that?

I just want to make sure you don't miss it.

Bones and More Bones

PIRATES HOOK

Sand and millions of living, breathing organisms line the sea floor. But at one point, in one spot on the bottom of the Caribbean Sea, skeletons walked. The pirates living under the ancient curse walked there under the waves. Their destination? The HMS Dauntless, a Royal Navy ship anchored offshore. The slimy, wet bones walked the ocean floor, planning to overtake the Navy ship.

Out of the deep, they climb aboard. An inequitable fight breaks out on the ship's deck—it's Navy vs. The Fighting Skeletons That Won't Die.

Meanwhile, back in the cave of treasures, Jack and Barbossa engage in a swordfight for honor and rule of the Black Pearl. Will, too, crosses blades with a few pirate stragglers that stayed behind.

His adversaries don't know that before the fight broke out Jack wormed his way up to the treasure chest filled with the gold medallions. Sly as a fox, Jack has *something up his sleeve. Literally—one of the Aztec gold medallions which he stole from the chest without Barbossa's knowledge. The medallion's an insurance policy, as it were.*

Will makes his way to the open treasure chest of gold. Slicing his palm with his sword, he catches the last medallion flying through the air from Jack's hand. The gold mixed with Will's blood will reverse the curse, bringing life back into the bones of the Black Pearl*'s crew.*

Seconds before the bloodied medallion lands in the treasure chest with the 881 other identical pieces, Jack uses his one bullet. He fires the lone shot into Barbossa's body.

As the gold piece clinks into the treasure chest, reunited with its kin, Barbossa and the other pirates find their bodies and feelings restored. The bones take on tendons and organs and flesh.

Unfortunately for the mutinous Captain Barbossa, Jack's bullet draws real blood—and real death—to the scalawag.

Barbossa's reign of terror is finished.

DISCOVERING THE TREASURE

It's hard to forget all those bones.

Were they alive? Well, yes and no. The skeletons did have some lifelike qualities—some contained tendons and maybe even a little flesh. After a while I realized they even had breath within them. They made quite an interesting gang.

So how did you react when you first saw the moving, lifelike bones attached by sinew? Maybe they didn't bother you at all. Some of you likely thought they were cool. I'm sure others were grossed out by them, while still others probably spent time studying them and dissecting every part of the scene, either because you were fascinated by its meaning or looking to find fault with it.

I myself found it fascinating. It reminded me of that scene in the *Pirates of the Caribbean* movie when the cursed pirates became walking bones—skeletons with lifelike qualities.

Wait—you thought that's what I was referring to in the first place? Oops, sorry. I'm talking about the bones in Ezekiel 37. (I guess I can see why you're confused.)

Let's check out the bones and skeletons the Old Testament prophet Ezekiel described. The Spirit of the Lord led Ezekiel ("Zeke" for short) into a valley full of bones. Unlike the wet pirate bones in the movie, these were very brittle, sun-dried bones.

The Lord then asked ol' Zeke if he thought the valley's dried-out bones could live. Now Zeke didn't just fall off the pomegranate cart; he wisely deferred back to the all-knowing, all-powerful God.

But instead of answering Zeke, God responded with action. (He's great at that, isn't He?) The Lord instructed the prophet to do what he did best—prophesy! So Zeke used the words Yahweh-God gave him: "I will make breath enter you, and you will come to life. I will attach tendons to you and make flesh come upon you and cover you with skin; I will put breath in you, and you will come to life. Then you will know that I am the LORD" (vv. 5–6).

Rumble, rumble, rumble. No, that's not Zeke's hungry stomach calling out. It was the dry valley bones—they started to shake, rattle, and roll. Then tendons, followed by flesh, appeared on them. What a sight! But something's not right. No breath in the bodies. Minor detail.

The Lord again put his words on Zeke's breath saying, "Come from the four winds, O breath, and breathe into these slain, that they may live" (v. 9). To no one's surprise, air filled their lungs and their hearts began to beat. They came to life and stood up (probably with perfect posture). They looked like a huge army!

God wasn't pulling Ezekiel's leg here. And it wasn't a ploy to get Ezekiel nominated for patron saint of chiropractors! God had a purpose in bringing these bones back to life.

The bones represented God's people, who had watched their hope vanish and their bones dry up in the hot desert sun of discouragement. The Lord told Zeke to inform the people that He wasn't going back on any promises. He had big plans to give them back their land and to breathe a Spirit-filled living hope into them as they stood confident in the Lord's power.

I guess walking bones aren't just found in pirate movies, huh? God's story through Ezekiel and the bones helps me stand up and stretch my body and my faith when my hope seems dried up and the marrow of discouragement runs through my bones.

Even my faith feels bone dry at times. You know what I mean, don't you? Sometimes it feels like...

- nobody will notice if you don't show up for work next week
- you can't connect with anyone at church
- you're the *Interceptor* and the *Black Pearl* is gaining ground on you
- your joy is missing in action
- the world has signed a pact with the devil (or, at the very least, a band of pilfering, plundering pirates)

- you're Elizabeth and your love seems out of reach
- you're trapped in a rut and getting a recorded message when you call 911
- your bones are drying up in a desert valley of guilt

I'm thinking it's a good time to have a talk with the Captain. Are you onboard with me?

Dear Captain, my Captain,
I love You, Lord, and I know You love me. If You find those truths living within me only as head knowledge, please reassign them to each chamber of my heart.

I desperately need for Your Holy Spirit to breathe a living hope within me. Fill my physical and spiritual lungs with new life—Your life. Then surround me with Your promises, so they become the constant air I breathe. Transform my dry bones of faithlessness with Christ's marrow of righteousness. Pump joy through my veins. Cause my joints to move in whatever direction You tell them. Teach my hands to release my grip on anything of the world and instead to hold tightly to the truth of Your Word and will.

Open my ears to clearly hear Your voice of compassion, correction, and forgiveness. Instruct my flesh to serve as Your instrument, holding my life together through Your life that lives within me.

Father, create. Flow through me, Savior. And breathe, Spirit, breathe life into me. May I stand humbly yet boldly before You, God, allowing You to penetrate every molecule of my being with Your living, breathing, transforming presence and promises. I stand before You praising You for giving Your life, Jesus, for me and for giving me life in Your treasured name. It's in that perfect name I pray and live. Amen.

Ye Opportune Moment

PIRATES HOOK

Elizabeth, Will, and Jack find themselves alone in the cavern. Their battle with Barbossa and his pirate goons is over. Jack concerns himself with the gold and silver while Will and Elizabeth concern themselves with each other.

They move closer and closer. A kiss is only a breath away...until Elizabeth dismisses the temptation and walks back toward the Dauntless.

Jack staggers over to Will, his hands filled with gold and a jeweled crown perched jauntily atop his head. He stares at Elizabeth's back as she walks away, then points out the obvious to poor Will:

"If you were waiting for the opportune moment... that was it."

DISCOVERING THE TREASURE

The writer of Ecclesiastes (likely Solomon) tells us that God made a time for everything—that there is an opportune moment and season for every activity under heaven.

He says God made…

…a time to be born and a time to die.

- At the divinely appointed opportune time on Christmas Eve, God blessed Sue and Jon with the gift of Abigail Christine. The birth of the Christ-child forever changed this family of four.
- On Christmas Eve, Leigh-Lane Edwards entered heaven. In God's perfect timing (although it may seem perfectly imperfect to us), this faith-filled twenty-year-old moved from her temporary, earthly home to her permanent, true home.
  The birth of Christ will never be the same for both families.

…a time to plant and a time to uproot.

- This week Amanda and Dustin uprooted themselves from apartment living and found themselves planted in their first home. Housewarming gifts of prayers arrived in heaven at the opportune moment. What a difference a Savior makes when He's invited into homes and lives.
- This week a farmer plants seeds and waits for God to miraculously bear fruit with them.
  In another part of the world, knowing the time is right, a farmer uproots potatoes. Taste and see the goodness of the Lord of the harvest.

...a time to kill and a time to heal.

- This morning a tribesman hid in the brush, spear in hand, waiting for the opportune moment to bring home dinner for his family. Oh give thanks to our Provider, for He is good.
- This morning a single mom underwent successful gall bladder surgery. Doctors report that quick and complete healing is expected. O give thanks for the best of care—found in the healing hands of the Great Physician.

...a time to tear down and a time to build.

- Over the weekend God helped Sally tear down a wall of bitterness between herself and her parents. Grace grew on both sides of the wall. On Monday, Sally's boss asked her to train a new employee. From the first few hours of working together, both young ladies sensed the building of a new friendship, thanks to the One who calls them friend.

...a time to weep and a time to laugh.

- A lonely housewife pulls her car to an abandoned area of a parking lot. Her heart throbs as she sobs. At just the right time, she feels the presence of Jesus. She leans into His embrace while He wipes her tears. His heart throbs for her as she sobs.

That night she and her family will spend time together eating, playing a game, and laughing together at a favorite *I Love Lucy* episode. Joy comes in the morning with Jesus.

.... a time to mourn and a time to dance.

- Bob mourns the loss of his job. Ruth mourns the loss of her eyesight due to macular degeneration. Sean mourns the death of his grandmother. Thankfully, at the opportune moment Jesus brings Good News in the midst of mourning on Easter morning.

- Marco dances with joy when his team wins the championship. Tears of joy dance down Mona's face when she receives news that her daughter is returning from the war. Oscar takes his bride of fifty years into his arms and leads her in an anniversary waltz. The joy of the Lord is our strength.

...a time to scatter stones and a time to gather them.

- Eli decides to enlist, convinced that this is a just war. Before signing, he rereads the account of David and Goliath in 1 Samuel 17. The battle is the Lord's.

- The Lord led his people into the Promised Land and instructed Joshua to have one person from each of the twelve tribes gather a large stone and place it in the Jordan as a permanent memorial to God's grace (Joshua 4). The victory belongs to the Lord.

...a time to embrace and a time to refrain.

- Mark embraces the good news, throws his arms around his wife, and rejoices with her. God is good…all the time.
- Finding herself in a possible compromising position, JoAnn realizes it is the right time to walk away. God is good…all the time.

...a time to search and a time to give up.

- Reggie seeks God's direction as he faces a weighty decision. He persists in his prayers for guidance and wisdom. Weeks later he feels the Lord leading him to change his request and refrain from asking for direction while continuing to rely on His wisdom. God continues to speak to His people.

...a time to keep and a time to throw away.

- With God's help, James holds onto God's promises. He returns to church, keeps his appointments with the counselor, and continues to hold on with the help of his accountability partner. With God's help, James is able to throw away tempting reminders of his past and the sin that so easily entangled him. Celebrate our Savior, who will never give up on us.

...a time to tear and a time to mend.

- Having lost everything, Job tore his tunic as a sign of mourning and sat in silence.
- Betty and Frank struggle for months and months, trying to deal with the reality of their prodigal son. A couple from church facing a similar situation strike up a friendship with them, and the couples help mend each other's broken hearts. Jesus comes to bind up the brokenhearted.

...a time to be silent and a time to speak.

- Suzanne waits in line at the funeral home, her mind searching to find the right words to say. As she approaches her grieving friend, they hold each other for minutes, neither saying a word. God blesses us with a ministry of presence.
- Seizing the opportune moment, a neighbor invites Paulo's mother over for a cup of coffee and an afternoon of sharing, crying, and laughing—exactly one month after her son died in a car accident. God's timing is perfect.

...a time to love and a time to hate.

- The opportune moment is now. "Love must be

sincere. Hate what is evil; cling to what is good"
(Romans 12:9).

- And so we know and rely on the love God has
for us. God is love. Whoever lives in love lives in
God, and God in him (1 John 4:16). Indeed, our
God is love.

...a time for war and a time for peace.

- Jesse knows his boss's request reeks of ethics vio-
lations. At a Spirit-directed moment, Jesse
decides to take a stand and confronts his boss.
He stands firm on his position. He loses his job,
but wins the battle for his Lord.
- The day overflows with interruptions, crises,
research, and basic mayhem. At an opportune
moment, Julie runs the water, locks the bath-
room door, soaks in a mountain of bubbles,
closes her eyes and prays. And rests. And rests
some more. At just the right time, God's Spirit
leads her eyes to the needlepoint message hanging on the wall: "Be still, and know that I am
God" (Psalm 46:10).

There's an opportune time to do things, a right
time for everything on the earth. (Ecclesiastes 3:1,
The Message)

You see, at just the right time, when we were still
powerless, Christ died for the ungodly. (Romans 5:6)

This is the opportune time for Jesus.

Someone's Come Between Us

PIRATES HOOK

The curse is lifted. The skirmish is over. The good guys have won. And of course, the boy gets the girl...eventually! Only one more skirmish remains to be had.

Royal sailors and townspeople alike fill the Port Royal courtyard. They're here to see Captain Jack Sparrow...and his impending demise by gallows.

Will finds himself pushing eagerly through that crowd. Far from being just a curious bystander, he has a twofold mission. First, he must tell Elizabeth he has loved her since the first time he set eyes on her—check that off his to-do list. Saving Jack's life is his second priority—check that off his list too. Thanks to his expertise with the sword, Will saves Jack's neck.

Yes, working as a team, Jack and Will clothesline one group of bayonet-carrying redcoats. Then they somersault past another. Fists and legs strike their blows. Some red-coated bodies double over; others fall to the ground as Jack and Will play the tag-team duo in Karate Kid meets WWF All-Stars.

But all good escape attempts must come to an end, and Jack and Will eventually find themselves encircled by bayonets.

Jack stands behind Will as Commodore Norrington comes over to gloat, a cocky, disgusted look on his face. Shocked at Will's turning on them, the Commodore and the Governor chastise him.

But the blacksmith with pirate blood in his veins defends Jack's honor, stating that his conscience will be clear, even if it brings him death.

Norrington steps toward Will. "You forget your place, Turner."

Boldly, Will responds, "It's right here, between you and Jack."

"As is mine," comes a voice from behind Norrington.

Elizabeth moves into the circle of bayonets, stepping between the Commodore and Jack, next to her one true love, Will Turner.

DISCOVERING THE TREASURE

I love theater. In high school I got the acting bug while performing scenes and monologues for area forensics competitions. In college I loved having more opportunities not only to act, but also to write a few plays and take courses in directing, lighting, and set design. These days, when a Broadway touring company comes to town, I love to head to the historic Fox

Theater and allow the show to carry me into another world for a few hours.

One of the first things I learned about acting is that before memorization or any acting takes place, the director blocks each scene with the cast. Blocking sets up the movement within a scene. An actor needs to learn not only lines, but also blocking. General rules (with some exceptions) include:

1. Know where to stand and when to move.
2. Don't turn your back to the audience.
3. Don't stand between another actor and the audience.

As the play runs smoothly, we in the audience never realize the role that smooth blocking plays in helping tell the story, drawing us into the scenes.

Although blocking still plays an important role in the production, rules for blocking movie or TV scenes differ from those onstage, since cameras shoot from any angle. Directors and cameramen carefully choose which angles to shoot from. They don't want to film the back of someone's head or the backs of actors walking out of the shot. The director's task in coordinating every aspect of the film is monumental.

In this *Pirates of the Caribbean* movie scene, the cameras first take a wider shot from the view of the audience, filming Norrington facing Will, with Jack hiding behind his newfound friend. Redcoats, with their bayonets pointed in the faces of Will and Jack after their ill-fated escape attempt, encircle the three.

The camera angle then switches, giving the audience a look at Will and Jack from Norrington's point of view. It then moves to another angle behind Jack and the redcoats.

When Norrington tells Will that he has forgotten his place, the director calls for a close-up of the Commodore's face. When Will responds with the words, "It's right here, between you and Jack," the camera zooms in for a close-up of the blacksmith with pirate's blood in his veins. Next, they move to a close-up of Elizabeth, revealing her look of gumption. And finally, they zoom out as she moves past Norrington and takes her rightful place next to her true love, Will.

The camera angle changes constantly, yet we pay little attention as we watch a movie or a TV show. Unbeknownst to us, these changing viewpoints play an important role in telling the production's story, adding effects and dramatization.

Unfortunately we in the audience also don't pay much attention to the divine *blocking* set up for us in heaven. Thankfully this blocking doesn't involve acting, while it does involve an action. Thankfully, this scene doesn't end in an hour or two; instead, it goes on forever…and rightly so!

The Director planned this scene way back in Act One, with Adam and Eve taking center stage and Satan, dressed in a serpent's costume, entering stage right and initiating a scandalous dialogue with the first lady of Eden. Its script may have looked *a little* like this:

SATAN: (*in serpent drag; to Eve*) Psst! (*or "Sssssss," if you're a method actor*) One of those little birdies told me that God told you not to eat from any tree in this beautiful garden paradise.

EVE: (*disgusted; moving in toward the serpent, shaking her finger*) Now see here, that's how rumors get started. Last week I heard through the grapevine that Adam wears the plants in this family, and that's just not true! And you have your story wrong too. God didn't say we couldn't eat from *any* tree. The memo I received gave strict instructions not to touch or to eat of the tree in the *middle* of the garden or we will die.

SATAN: Surely, you will not die, matey.

EVE: Quit calling me Shirley. Savvy?

SATAN: Surely—I mean, Eve—ya'll won't die. Excuse me, I be spendin' a lot of time lately in the south'rn part of the garden.

EVE: (*thinking, sitting down on what she thinks is a rock but is actually the shell of a giant tortoise*) So, you're saying God won't quibble if we nibble a little?

(*Tortoise gets up and quickly exits stage right as Eve stands.*)

SATAN: God must think you were born yesterday! Aye, ye won't die; so don't be shy! He knows if you eat the fruit of the tree you'll have godlike insights. You'll know all the details—the good, the bad, and the ugly. Come on, Eve, why put off until tomorrow what you can chew today? Savvy?

The scene ends with the fruit-of-the-doom Adam and Eve exiting stage left, desperately seeking a pair of Fruit-of-the-Looms. (*The tortoise continues to hurry off stage right but lags behind when he must stop to catch his breath.*) And with that the curtain closes on paradise…well, sort of.

Let's jump to another scene. It's tempting to refer to it as the *last* scene. But this true story lasts and lasts; it's the *real* neverending Story. Enter through your mind (and the truths of Scripture) into heaven's paradise.

The scene opens with people from every tribe and nation facing center stage where Jesus Christ, the second person of the Trinity, true God and true man, the world's Savior, the promised Messiah, the Rock of our Salvation, the Hope and Light of the World, the Resurrected, Living, and Eternal Lord takes His place. Special lighting is unnecessary as His glory fills every inch of heaven's boundless stage. The blocking for His angels simply calls for all of them to surround the Lord, while their script calls for them to continually worship.

Then Jesus, the One given all authority in heaven and earth, separates the people, one group stage right and another stage left. Cue God's faithful to stand at His right. And cue those who decided to reject His gifts of faith and life to stand downstage left.

The faces and body language of those waiting for their banishment from the presence of the Lord indicate that they know they're getting what they deserve, but that their realization has come too late.

JESUS: (*turning and looking at those on his left*) Depart from me, you who are cursed, into the eternal fire prepared for the devil and his angels (Matthew 25:41).

Given their cue, the billions of Jesus-rejecters turn and exit stage left as a final curtain separating them from the Lord closes after they depart, shutting out all their hopes of paradise.

Upstage, downstage, and center stage right overflow with billions of Christ-followers. Their faces and body language tell the story of a humbled group who know that they find themselves still part of the cast because they've been saved from rejection by grace through faith in Jesus Christ. It's obvious they didn't get there on their own. Right before our eyes a salvation miracle takes place. (It's not a staged miracle—it's the real thing!) Each one seems to have taken on a Jack Sparrow–like role. Found guilty of breaking every law, they know they deserve eternal death in the fires of hell. But thankfully, the Director has chosen surprising blocking and unique dialogue; He calls for all to take their positions.

A group of Baptist choir members begin humming "When the Roll Is Called up Yonder." Then a group of Lutherans walk to the Pearly Gates, where they nail a piece of paper that includes ninety-five statements—each including a recipe for "Grace-Alone Noodles 'n' Chicken Casserole." And a group of Presbyterians place "John 3:16" signs into the raised hands of the Pentecostals.

Then your name is called up yonder, followed by mine. We remember the blocking, walking toward God's throne of grace. We stand in silence—momentarily speechless in His presence. We stand in silence, knowing we have no defense for our sin-saturated lives.

ANGEL: (*loudly proclaiming the words of Romans 8:1*)
Therefore, there is now no condemnation for those who are in Christ Jesus.

(*Center stage, Jesus stands between us and the Father.*)

JESUS: Father, I take my place before You. Tim and (*your name here*) stand behind me. I ask that You judge their imperfect, sinful, and death-deserving lives by My perfect life and sacrifice for their sins. I gracefully cover them with My righteousness. I washed their robes in My blood, shed when I gave

My life for them on the cross outside Jerusalem. I gave My life for them so they could live. They did not quench the power of the Spirit as faith was gifted to them. I love My children. Judge them, Father, on My perfection and not on their imperfection.

GOD THE FATHER, GOD THE SON, AND GOD THE HOLY SPIRIT: *(boldly, joyfully, and in one voice)* NOT GUILTY! Welcome to paradise!

JESUS: *(quoting His own words recorded in Matthew 25:34)* Come, you who are blessed by my Father; take your inheritance, the kingdom prepared for you since the creation of the world.

(The story continues…eternally…all because Someone came between us and the Father.)

But God demonstrates his own love for us in this: While we were still sinners, Christ died for us. Since we have now been justified by his blood, how much more shall we be saved from God's wrath through him! For if, when we were God's enemies, we were reconciled to him through the death of his Son, how much more, having been reconciled, shall we be saved through his life! (Romans 5:8–10)

> Amazing Script(ure)!
> Perfectly written dialogue!
> Performances out of this world!
> Divine blocking!
> And there's no admission charge!
> Don't miss His story…coming soon to a life near you!

Where Does Your Heart Lie?

PIRATES HOOK

Surrounded by redcoats wielding bayonets, Will boldly takes his place between the Commodore and Captain Jack Sparrow. Able to go forth with a clear conscience, Will pledges allegiance to his defensive position.

Stepping out of her father's shadow, Elizabeth bravely enters the circle of guns and swords and positions herself next to Will, her heart's desire. Commodore Norrington, her forced-faux-fiancé, looks her in the eyes and asks, "So this is where your heart truly lies, then?"

She responds without hesitation. "It is."

DISCOVERING THE TREASURE

"So this is where your heart truly lies, then?"

The answer seemed to settle within me. It's not an easy question. It looks and sounds like it's calling for a simple, obvious answer…but it's not.

"So this is where your heart truly lies, then?"

Suddenly I realized that all the pirates and redcoats had double-edged swords. The sword imagery took me straight to the New Testament.

> For the word of God is living and active. Sharper than any double-edged sword, it penetrates even to dividing soul and spirit, joints and marrow; it judges the thoughts and attitudes of the heart. Nothing in all creation is hidden from God's sight. Everything is uncovered and laid bare before the eyes of him to whom we must give account. (Hebrews 4:12–13)

My answer was right there in front of me. Any closer and it would have singed me!

The living, active word of God lays open the thoughts and attitudes of the heart. Maybe unconsciously the idea of a sword plunging into my living, active heart didn't exactly thrill me. I'm not good when it comes to pain. But then again, pain wouldn't make anyone's top ten list of things to look forward to (dart boards and pin cushions excluded).

But this pain is different from the pain I experienced this morning when I received a tetanus shot. The pain that comes from one edge of the sword creates a dull, aching pain called guilt. It makes consciences throb, guts churn, and focal points blur. It forces us to look over our shoulders at our past. Paranoid, we check out what lurks around every corner. Shameful, we hang our heads, unable to look others in the eye.

So where does my heart lie? Well, I honestly have to say that it's divided. I want so badly to look my Jesus in the eye and say with complete faithfulness, "I love you with all my heart, mind, strength, and soul. I give you my entire heart and being. Every breath I take I breathe in Your life."

If I said *that*, the question should read, "When does my heart *lie*?"

Yes! With you—this is where my heart truly lies! I want to shout that, sing that, pray that, live that! But one edge of the swordlike Word tells me less than 100 percent of my heart beats in sync with His. Do you know how difficult it is to admit that? To acknowledge it outright? To print it here in full view when asked, "Where does my heart lie?"

Can I answer…with Jesus? That's where my heart *does* lie, isn't it?

Yes, but not fully. Not completely.

Jesus once had a conversation with a law expert about this very matter.

On one occasion an expert in the law stood up to test Jesus. "Teacher," he asked, "what must I do to inherit eternal life?"

"What is written in the Law?" he replied. "How do you read it?"

He answered: "'Love the Lord your God with all your heart and with all your soul and with all your strength and with all your mind'; and, 'Love your neighbor as yourself.'"

"You have answered correctly," Jesus replied. "Do this and you will live." (Luke 10:25–28)

Oh, that's all? Why didn't you say so earlier? That's ALL? "Do this and you will live"? I feel like screaming—like a pirate: "AARRRGGHHHHH!"

Another time, when a rich young man asked Jesus the same question, He simply walked him through the commandments. The man insisted he'd been keeping those since he was a boy. Then come the inspired words: "Jesus looked at him and loved him" (Mark 10:21).

Jesus looked at him and loved him.

Jesus looked at him and loved him.

I love that.

Maybe I love His actions so much because I'm thinking that if Jesus responded in that way to the young man in front of Him, it's just possible, maybe even probable, that He would do the same for this not-so-young man in front of Him right now, as well as for you.

Jesus looks at me and loves me. Say that out loud. Go ahead. He looks at *you* and loves *you*.

Jesus looks at us and loves us...even when our hearts are divided. Not that He loves that our hearts are fractured—in fact, He hates the sin that divides hearts. But He still loves us.

Jesus looks at us and loves us. That look. That love. It makes us want to harmonize with David, "Teach me your way, O LORD, and I will walk in your truth; give me an undivided heart, that I may fear your name" (Psalm 86:11).

An undivided heart. No, not a *sword of* undivided heart. A complete, forgiven, full, undivided heart.

What? You don't think He's going to put His blood-stained stamp of approval on the request? He will, *but*...well, let me explain.

The undivided hearts we desire won't come to fruition until we arrive *home* and the church—Christ's bride on earth—births us from death to life into the nail-scarred hands of Jesus, the Bridegroom.

He'll carry us into the presence of souls of Christ-followers from every tribe and nation—from Greenland to Greensboro; from the Poles to Poland; from Austria to Australia; from Taipei to Tiparari; from Savannah to the Sahara; from the Orient to Oakville.

And in the language of heaven, they'll welcome us with shouts of joy, heavenly high fives, songs of joy, and standing ovations—not for us, but for our Savior, who made this gift of heaven possible. Even angels will harmonize as our Savior rejoices over us with singing while our entire being cries out in praise to our Mansion Builder, our righteous Garment Designer, our Grace Giver. Then, and only then, will our hearts, our attention, and our praise be undivided.

Until Jesus peels back layers of the universe, revealing heaven and bringing us into paradise, we can't possibly live with perfectly undivided hearts.

But hold on. That double-edged sword of the Word…we're starting to see the other side, aren't we? We experienced the pain of sin and guilt in our lives. Our divided hearts are exposed. We confessed our sins. Now we humbly accept His complete forgiveness.

And He offers us a glimpse into the day when it becomes an impossibility for His children to live with those divided hearts. His Word pierced our being like a sword thrust into flesh, and we experienced the pain of our sin.

But His Word also has a healing side. He looks at us and loves us. Ahhhh, the gospel—the Good News. Forgiveness. Healing. Sword extraction. Salvation. Hope.

The double-edged sword of the Word…His law and His gospel. We need both. Without the law, we'd have no need for the gospel and our Savior's saving act of love. Without the gospel, hope wouldn't exist. We would fail with no possibility of forgiveness or heaven.

Jesus looks at us and loves us.

That's where His heart lies.

As we confess the causes for the divisions within us, the mutinies we've initiated, and the failures to make Satan walk the plank, we find that our hearts lie within the undivided heart of Jesus.

His heart envelops ours.

Our hearts *do* lie undivided within the perfect heart of Jesus.

Our hearts—louder and louder—begin to rhythmically beat in sync with His.

Our hearts began to beat with more vigor when Jesus' heart flatlined as His lungs took in their last bit of Golgotha air while pinned to a cross-shaped tree.

Our hearts began to pump His blood through our bodies with a stronger and livelier beat one Sunday when His lungs filled with resurrection air.

Our hearts…alive and well.

Our hearts.

His heart.

One heart.

One hope.

———————

So this is where your heart truly lies, then—with Jesus?

It is.

Not *sword of*… It is!

So this is where your heart truly lies, then?

It is…in Him, with Him, and through Him.

So this is where your heart truly lies, then?

It is…only because He looked at you and loved you.

Now, Bring Me That Horizon

PIRATES HOOK

Reinstated as captain of the Black Pearl, *Jack Sparrow stands proudly at the ship's wheel. His dark, wavy hair flows from under his well-worn tricorn hat down onto his shoulders. He gazes over the calm Caribbean waters and says with satisfaction, "Now, bring me that horizon."*

DISCOVERING THE TREASURE

I looked for the Caribbean horizon as I drove down the interstate today.

Unfortunately, it's kind of hard to see that point where sky and earth meet when you're driving on city streets, surrounded by houses, buildings, and trees. Because of this, I don't generally use the horizon as my point of reference.

But for a pirate like Captain Jack Sparrow, horizons are benchmarks.

Four days from now I'll have an entirely different view. I'll actually see the horizon stretching across Caribbean waters! I'm not vacationing in the Caribbean, nor will I sail on a pirate ship (at least not deliberately). I'm part of a group of eleven men and women from our church who will soon board a plane, surrounded by prayers and God's promised-filled presence, and embark on a mission trip to the Caribbean island of Trinidad.

We've been invited to minister to prisoners, share in various ways with school children, and hold a Vacation Bible School during our short-term, eight-day mission trip.

At this time, my anticipation of horizon viewing is limited. I've heard about the gigantic Hindu monkey-faced godhead statue that's eighty-five feet tall. The life-size elephant statues flown in from India that stand at the entrances of a meditation center dedicated to a Hindu god also pique my interest. I've also heard stories about the fire ants that seem to rule the ground where we'll be sharing the saving news of Jesus Christ.

Why does my horizon-viewing anticipation seem to stop at the ants and the giant monkey idol? I don't like fire ants. As for giant monkeys, well, I've never seen one in person, but it seems like it might be a little intimidating.

I can't imagine that I'm the only one who focuses on self-centered concerns instead of looking for the horizons fashioned by our creative, unlimited God. It's so easy to gaze at limited horizons that are nothing more than optical illusions playing games with our eyes of faith.

Think about it. Since we can't see into the future, our weak faith sees as a limiting factor the line at which the sky and earth appear to meet. We do know that the world isn't flat, right? I'll double-check my research on that one, but I think I'm safe in stating that.

We limit our faith vision. Like a sponge, absorb these horizon-breaking words…

> Jesus said, "You're tied down to the mundane; I'm in touch with what is beyond your horizons. You live in terms of what you see and touch. I'm living on other terms. I told you that you were missing God in all this. You're at a dead end. If you won't believe I am who I say I am, you're at the dead end of sins. You're missing God in your lives." (John 8:23–24, *The Message*)

While probably an overused spiritual cliché, we do try to fit God in a box—one constructed of warped plywood. Our finite minds can't handle the truth that the one true God—Father, Son, and Holy Spirit—is infinite.

Consider for example your last time spent in hot water (figuratively speaking). Did you expect God to help you? Pray for God to help you?

We often have such low expectations. Do we think the hot water will shrink the miraculous rescue-strength of our all-knowing, all-powerful, present-everywhere Savior-God? Our Jesus is in touch with what's beyond our horizons, no matter how hot the water or how intimidating the wind and waves.

> A small rudder on a huge ship in the hands of a skilled captain sets a course in the face of the strongest winds. (James 3:4, *The Message*)

We have a God who is in touch with what's beyond our horizons. When we live with weakened eyes of faith, we may think the horizon ends when...

- we clock out at work or hear the last school bell
- the word *cancer* slips out during a conversation with the doctor
- the storm hits town
- the hard drive crashes
- the funeral director asks which casket we'd like to use
- the divorce papers arrive
- a bankruptcy sign flashes in the back of our minds
- the rejection letter arrives
- we don't make the final cut
- the tow truck backs up to the car
- we walk the plank, or head in a new direction, blindfolded
- we remember Jesus' death on the cross

Jesus Christ, our Savior and Lord, is in touch with what lies beyond our limited and untrusting horizons. Nothing escapes Him. Nothing happens without His knowledge. Nothing is too far from His reach or His grace.

God the Father didn't set a limited horizon beyond the cross where Jesus breathed His last. However, the disciples couldn't see past it. Neither could the women. The same story applied to so many of His followers. But our living God even saw beyond the horizon of death.

About a dozen chapters ago I introduced you to Leigh-Lane Edwards, my son's college friend who passed beyond the horizon of the life we see. She received the gift of heaven at the age of twenty and will never again leave her home. Her death (and entrance to heaven) shocked everyone. Leigh-Lane knew how to live, however…because she knew her living Savior. She had no warning. No time to say, "I'll see you in heaven." No time for one last "I love you" before an unexpected aneurysm exploded in her aorta on Christmas Eve.

Leigh-Lane knew her Savior was in touch with what lay beyond her limited horizon. She trusted her horizon-exploding Lord completely. You want to know how I know? She told me, through an entry in her journal of conversations with her living Jesus. Nine months before she entered heaven, Leigh-Lane sat in a café and wrote in her journal. Incomplete sentences. Random thoughts. Love notes. When Leigh-Lane wrote the words, she didn't have a clue she'd soon pass beyond earth's horizon. Her words cry out with trust in the only One who knew what lay beyond the horizon of the next minute, let alone the horizon of her short twenty years on earth. As you read her entry, the obvious will come to light. Leigh-Lane was in love…with Jesus. And Jesus was crazy in love with Leigh-Lane.

Sing a song so sweet 3.8.05

The Lord is my strength so beautiful like flowers blooming and the gentle fall of rain in the spring. The clouds are the best after a storm; maybe life is like that too. Art shows, Spanish newspapers… and not knowing what tomorrow holds. Thankful for the Lord, the strength of my life, all fullness and joy is in Him, Him alone. Me, my benefit of His grace is all so amazing, such joy and thankfulness triumphs over sadness and sorrow, I know who wins, I know my Redeemer lives, I know my steps are ordered and He is by my side; I will not be shaken, my rock, my fortress. A wellspring of creativity and surprise, He leads me alongside still waters, He directs my steps, protects me so even my foot won't stumble. I know He is with me, His peace is here. He is altogether trustworthy and I have no worries, for He is in control. His love is amazing. So blessed, seeing the spark of love in a child playing with her toes and in a husband and wife picking out some photography and the selfless love of caring for an elderly mother. How amazing, how he looks in her eyes now they're engaged, a sleigh ride and a hope for the future in Christ. Something is so amazing. Thank You for letting me see a glimpse of Your love in people. How amazing, may I serve and be a blessing and selfless and just be found in Christ. Know where my strength comes from, my joy, my peace. Lord, how great is Your Name, You are altogether lovely and faithful, always faithful to this ragamuffin child full of big dreams, and scraped knees and an easily distracted ear, prone to wander, Lord I feel it, but may my eyes ever go up to Your throne. And may I know so much more what is the height and depth and width of Your love for me, what love is, what the Gospel is, and grace oh to know the wonders of grace. How amazing, Lord, thank You for letting me know,

if even just for a little while that Your love
endures forever for all time, for all challenges.
...Beautiful in this place, this coffee shop where no one
knows where I am facing the window so I can pretend
I am alone in here, thankful for little secrets I can
keep, little moments when it's just You and me,
may I crave more and more of those. Your peace
flows amidst all the hustle and bustle, the busy-ness
and the people...always the people. What a chance to
show love. Give my life for what seems like love.

—Leigh Lane Edwards

Jesus, don't allow me to limit my faith horizons. Grace me, Spirit, with a faith like Leigh-Lane's. Take me beyond Your neverending horizons. It's time to set sail, Jesus. Standing at the ship's wheel, I can hear you say, "You're tied down to the mundane; I'm in touch with what is beyond your horizons. You live in terms of what you see and touch. I'm living on other terms (John 8:23, *The Message*).

Now, bring me that horizon!

On second thought, bring me Jesus, who's in touch with what lies beyond my horizons.

Now, Spirit of God, bring me a faith that trusts Jesus' vision that lies way beyond my limited horizons.

Standing on the deck of Your grace, Jesus, I'm ready to set sail.

I'm ready, Jesus... *Captain* Jesus, my Captain.

Epilogue

When Jack believes he's safe and saved, he makes plans to get on with his pirate's life. He moves beyond Norrington, the redcoats, and a row of bayonets. He staggers toward Elizabeth's father, the Governor of Port Royal. Face-to-face with the Governor, Jack spews out some great lines. "Well! I'm feeling rather good about this. I think we've all arrived at a very special place. Aye? Spiritually. Ecumenically. Grammatically."

As I set anchor on this book, I think I can also say that I'm feeling rather good about this. I think we've arrived at a very special place. Aye? Spiritually. Ecumenically. And grammatically.

Thanks for joining me on this journey of exploration for treasure, mates! I hope you were blessed as *the* Captain brought us safely to this point, riding with us on the waves of grace, offering us a treasure trove of priceless gems found in His Word.

This isn't the end.

The adventure continues as we sail into every new day. Savvy?